Lift her up, tenderly

by Bob LeFevre

PINE TREE PRESS

DEDICATION

To Virginia, with fond and affectionate memories.

CONTENTS

INTRODUCTION

This is a textbook. It is designed to serve as the scaffolding around which a course in basic economics can be provided for students. Educators may possibly view it as a novel. Certainly, it is novel to discover a text about economics which contains human drama and emotion. The text is interesting. That contradicts all prior theories about economics.

Ever since Carlyle thundered his melancholy maledictions against the "gloomy science," scholars have reacted as though Carlyle were right. I think he was wrong. Without realizing it, Carlyle was probably reacting against the way economics is usually taught. If so, I can readily understand his pessimism and find myself equally uninspired.

All economic ideas are basically simple. That, in itself, may provide part of the difficulty economists have concerning the teaching of those ideas. After all, an economist is a human being and wishes to be respected and admired. How much respect and admiration will he engender if it is discovered that the course he teaches is so fundamentally simple that even children will readily understand it? Few persons holding doctoral degrees could attract the awe of the uninformed by interpreting Mother Goose.

In more than twenty years of studying and teaching economics, I have usually found that economic ideas which are really little more than common sense have been cloaked in such profundity that the discipline appears to be esoteric, abstruse, and far too difficult for the average adult to fully comprehend. However, if one will persist in probing the pedants who have constructed the most obtuse and convoluted definitions, one emerges finally with the realization that economics is something which could be taught in grade and high schools, while the student is quite young.

Let me provide an example. One economist has been receiving public recognition for his discovery of "demonstrated preference." Doesn't that sound impressive? What does it mean? It means that people often tell you something but act in a contrary manner. The point is that "actions speak louder than words," the old adage that anybody can understand. But who, without an interpreter, will immediately grasp that the ponderous, obfuscatory statement which sets forth the principle of "demonstration of preferences" means the same thing?

Then we have the earth-shaking theory of "marginal utility." This is such an important discovery that when it was first introduced, it virtually revolutionized the classic approach to economics. What it means is that people tend to favor those useful things which are most difficult to get. That could be summed up as "Easy come, easy go" plus "Hard to come by, bitter to lose." I did that last one myself because adages are fairly easy to construct and anyone can readily grasp the meaning.

In the United States, for many years emphasis has been placed on the physical sciences, technologies of various sorts, and supportive disciplines. The humanities and social studies have been either downgraded or construed into a kind of political format which virtually demands that the growing child submit all his problems to democratic decision-making. Before the youngster graduates from the grades, he has come to believe that he can get anything he wants if only he is popular enough and has a following. The verities of life are replaced by the processes of balloting. The values that make life worth living are shunted aside in favor of arrogant or submissive assurance that the numbers game governs all.

The formal teaching of economics has, unfortunately, tended to pursue this same direction. I am not seeking to downgrade or decry the importance of mathematical data nor the obvious usefulness of mathematical probabilities. What I am seeking to emphasize is that human values and common sense must take precedence. The basics ought to be taught to young people. And they should be taught in the home and in the early years in school. After such a foundation is laid, there's time enough for the computer.

Lift Her Up, Tenderly is pure fiction. A man in his fifties is the guardian of a twelve-year-old girl. The situations and dialogue are entirely imaginary. But the laws of economics (common sense) are suggested by the guardian and applied by the young lady in her efforts to deal with real life situations. I was influenced in preparing this text by my own experience in which I acted as an unofficial guardian for a young lady. Yes, there is a real Virginia.

My hope is that teachers will make use of this simple approach to economics and offer it as a course of study to young people in high school, or even in the grades.

Even more importantly, I hope that in its pages parents will rediscover the exciting and rewarding task of teaching their own children. Love alone is not enough. Physical maintenance, paying the bills, playing together — none of these is enough. Learning the meaning and common sense of living is a life-long challenge for parents and children alike.

To the young people who may read these pages, I would urge patience. Your parents really do love you. They may or may not be technically skilled, they may or may not be rich, or famous, or applauded, but the living of life contains great values that can never be found by measuring and computing, by tallying votes, or by popularity contests. And you have many things to teach them, too. The learning process is always mutual.

Bob LeFevre
California, 1976

Chapter 1

FAIR AND UNEQUAL

Virginia appeared at the door of my study. She stared at me, demanding my attention. I knew she was there, but I was working on my notes for a speech and I didn't look up. She knew I was aware of her. Any twelve-year-old, and most especially a twelve-year-old girl, has some inner mechanism which glows pleasantly when someone is thinking about her. Virginia's face revealed that her awareness mechanism had turned on. My concentration had been breached. She was inside my mind. I saw her smile as she decided to wait me out, one hand against the door jamb.

I relented. "All right, Gigi. Come in. I do have some work to do, but I'm glad to see you, all the same."

"You said you would always be available." She danced over to my chair and one small hand touched my sleeve affectionately. " 'Always' means all the time. So you have to talk to me all the time."

I regarded this feminine invasive force, marveling how anyone could shatter my concentration with such ease. Virginia was petite. Dark, shoulder-length hair framed an oval face, soft with the innocence of childhood. Her eyes were bright, sparkling with the look of knowing oh, so very much. The pupils were dark agates, and her face was unmarred by failure. My wife, Loy, and I were guardians. Virginia was all the more dear to us.

She was wearing her school clothes, blue skirt ending just above her knees, white blouse billowing around her arms and leaving generous space for growth of budding breasts. Her legs were bare except for white ankle-socks, and her shoes were square-toed, low-heeled oxfords.

"What do you want to talk about?" I asked.

"Oh, I don't know. Anything."

"Something bothering you?"

"No."

Her expression became vague and I interpreted it as cloaking a specific. I waited.

"Well, aren't you going to start?"

"Virginia, I have my mind on other things. But if you have a problem, I'll be glad to discuss it."

"Well, gosh all Friday. I don't have a problem. Gee! I don't see why you always think I have a problem."

"Okay. Then *I* have a problem. You see, I have to make this speech and. . . . "

"I'm tired of watching television."

"That's understandable."

"It's dumb. I don't see why people don't talk any more. I mean, why can't we have a conversation? Don't people have a conversation any more?"

"You know, hon, you've got a point. This modern society of ours isn't noted for its conversations. With all the mass-communication media available, we often let the professionals do our talking for us."

"It's boring, boring, boring."

I nodded. Was this the generation gap? How does a man in his fifties talk to a pre-teenage girl? The tendency is to instruct, to talk down, to pontificate. One is immediately filled with a realization of his own experience, his expertise, his knowledge. Is it fear that holds our tongues? Do we hesitate because we are afraid of being misunderstood? Are we hypersensitive to the knowledge that the mind before us is enormously sensitive, capable of being profoundly influenced? Or is it the reverse? Do we fear a lack of ability to influence?

Is it because we are desperately aware that time is on the side of youth? And being thus aware, do we long for recognition, acceptance by the young? Do we want to take command of the young life to help it escape the pitfalls we know all too well? Or do we want to be loved, most particularly by those so new to love?

"Are you bored, Virginia?"

The hair swirled and jounced an emphatic affirmative.

"Don't you think my conversation might be boring?"

I meant it teasingly, but she considered the point seriously. "I could let you know."

I recovered. "Do you know why I hesitate? I would absolutely hate boring you."

"Well, holy socks, you can't possibly bore me as much as TV. You simply can't."

I pivoted and she stepped closer, her sturdy leg in contact with my knee. "Papa, I'll tell you why TV bores me. They talk down. All the time. Like we were children. You don't do that."

"I don't?"

"Well. . . . " She hesitated. "Sometimes you do. But you can be terribly, terribly interesting, all the same. Papa, I want to know about life. The TV twirps at you all the time about nothing. They make a big deal about some little old trivial thing. They're always getting people up there to ask questions at. Like, how do you think the elections will turn out? And what did it mean when you first got a job? And how did you react when you made a home run or the fire broke out or something? Golly, I don't care about all that stuff. I want to know about life."

"Nobody knows all about life."

"You do."

"My dear, sweet girl. That's one of the most flattering things you've ever said. But it's false."

"No, it isn't. Sometimes you say things that really get me to thinking. You kind of put it all together so it makes sense."

One part of my mind accepted the praise. But this was dangerous ground. Why should I warm to such flattery?

"Virginia, help me over a couple of rough spots, will you? Nobody likes a know-it-all. Fortunately, I don't qualify. Nobody does. But if I start making positive statements, you could resent it. Haven't you noticed? Today, we have antiheroes; our hearts go out to the dummies, the bunglers, the impoverished, and even the vicious. People who give the appearance of knowing and then act successfully make many people uneasy. Today's villains are those who hold executive jobs, who make a better than average living, or who own substantial amounts of property. If I'm going to talk to you about life, I would want to talk to you about successful living. But I don't want to be a villain. And I don't want you to be one, either."

Those bright eyes bored into mine. "But that's just what I mean, Papa. I know about that." Excitement shook her voice. "At school all the time, they tell me about how I should fit in and try to get along. But I want my life to be special. I don't want to fit in." She looked startled. "No, I don't really mean how that sounded. I mean I want to do more than just fit in. I want to be a *person*."

She flung out her arms dramatically and I caught one tiny hand, holding it in my bigger one.

"Then, Virginia, we can talk. I'm going to forget any gap in age between us. I really do believe that I can be helpful. I'll try to be honest. But you must keep in mind that I can be mistaken. So I want you to challenge me if you think I'm off base. So, as of this minute, we're the same age. Okay? And we'll have a man to . . . man to woman talk. Okay?"

Virginia bounced up and down on her tiptoes, clapping her hands.

"Oh, thank you, Papa." She dashed across my study and began to worry a chair over to a place beside mine. "Don't start yet. Wait until I'm all ready."

"I think I'm a very fortunate guardian," I said, "to have a girl . . . a young woman in my home who wants to learn important, serious things. You know, Gigi, that's an interesting thing in itself. Most of us adults have the impression that young people today aren't really interested in serious things; that all they want is fun and games."

"I know, Papa. And it makes me so mad." She sat, one leg under her, the other swinging free. "Lots of the kids feel the same way. Nobody takes us serious. Parents keep dodging everything." She puckered her face. " 'You're too young to understand that, dear,' " she mimicked. " 'Later, when you're older.' 'Why don't you ask your teacher about that?' "

I laughed. "Say, you do that well. You're an accomplished actress."

"Do you think so, Papa?" She was pleased.

"In trying to marshal my ideas," I said, "I've suddenly remembered something. A very long time ago, a famous philosopher wrote about some pretty basic thoughts. In order to develop his ideas, he presented them in dialogue form. His name was Plato and he wrote about Socrates, who had a most interesting conversation with a group of young men."

Virginia nodded. "You mean Plato's *Republic*. I've read it."

I stared at her. "You've read Plato's *Republic*?"

"Of course. It was outside reading. I got it from the school library a long time ago."

"Did you read it all?"

"Of course."

"Did you like it? What did you think of it?"

"Well, I didn't understand it all. Golly, the sentences are long, kind of doubled up part of the time. But it's about justice and things like that."

"Maybe we ought to reverse our roles. Maybe you should be telling me about life."

She thought about that. "We could take turns," she suggested. "You can tell me first and then I can tell you."

"That appears to be reasonable." It took me a moment to refocus. "Back in those earlier times, conversation, dialogue, seemed a very good way to communicate ideas. I think it still is."

"Oh, it is, Papa. We do it at school a lot."

"Good. Then I'm beginning to catch on. I think there are two main areas of human living that we have to understand. One is the physical area; the other, the mental area. Both are vital and both can be interesting. And if we're going to have successful, full lives, we have to learn how to operate in both areas."

"What about the spiritual, Papa?"

"Spiritual things are part of the mental package, as I see it, Virginia. They involve belief, conviction, emotion. And there's a difference between religion and spirit. Religion is usually an organized set of theological ideas. Spiritual could mean enthusiasm, dedication, love, nobility, and lots of things like that. Perhaps we can talk about religion some other time. But I'd like to begin by confining our discussion to the physical side and to the mental area, which includes what we know and what we feel and believe. In a sense, we have to learn about both mental and physical areas at the same time. Economic understanding, in the sense I mean, is about the best common sense approach to life I know."

"What's economic understanding?"

"What does it sound like, Gigi?"

"It sounds icky."

"What's icky?"

"Yuk!"

"What's yuk?"

She screwed up her face. "Yuk is icky."

"I see." Chuckling, I said, "I think you're changing the pronunciation. Why don't we look it up? The word is *economics*, not icky-nomics. But a great many people would agree with the way you've said it. They think the subject is unpleasant, disagreeable, hard."

My *Webster's* showed the word pronounced *ee-ko-nom-iks* or *ek-o-nom-iks*. She looked to where my finger pointed in the open book.

"All right, then," she said. "Eekonomiks. What is it?"

"*Webster's* says: 'The science that investigates the conditions and laws affecting the production, distribution, and consumption of wealth, or the material means of satisfying human desires.' "

"What does that mean?"

"I guess we could say that economics is the study of how we make or obtain the material things that we must have in order to stay alive."

She thought about that. "Then it would be pretty important, wouldn't it, Papa?"

"Yes, indeed. It's rather basic."

"Then it's about life." She frowned. "I remember my teacher mentioned it once. She said that when I go to college, I might want to study it."

"You'll have to finish high school first."

"Well, of course. I know that." She sighed. "But it's pretty dumb. Here I am ready to study economics and they're so dumb they want me to finish high school first."

"I'm inclined to agree with you, my dear. Still, I think

you'll agree that many boys and girls aren't quite as mature as I'm sure you are. So the system of grade school, high school, and college has been set up that way for the benefit of the vast majority. So, maybe they aren't so dumb after all."

"It's not fair. I'm not the vast majority. I'm just me. Why can't I study economics now instead of waiting for college?"

"Actually, I think you should. And I believe in some schools a beginning is made even in the grades. I think that's a good thing. After all, Virginia, whatever you decide to do with your life, you are a material being. You live in a material world. And while I wouldn't want you to be dominated and overpowered by material things, you do have to deal with them all the time. As I said, economics is quite basic. To understand about life, it's a good place to start."

"Do you think I could understand it, Papa?"

"Oh, yes, of course. No question at all. I think most young people would understand it very well."

"Does it have anything to do with arithmetic? Math?"

"Well yes, and no."

She laughed at that. "It can't be both yes and no, Papa. You told me that yesterday."

"So I did."

"If it has anything to do with arithmetic, I don't want to study it. I hate math. It isn't about life. It's dead."

"Let me try to explain what I mean. Actually, economic study is the study of praxeology—the study of human action in the market place—and really isn't directly connected with arithmetic. But most economists rely on the language of mathematics in order to discuss economic ideas."

"Papa, you're using big words."

"I'll try to be more careful," I assured her. "Actually, economic rules are quite simple and easy to understand. You know, Gigi, I think economists have a tendency to take very simple ideas and then dress them up in such verbal finery that they sound profound."

"Are you an economist?"

"No, I'm just a teacher."

"Then why do you do the same thing? With words, I mean?"

"Habit, I suppose. Probably because we all want to be

respected. And we're a little self-conscious. If we spoke with simplicity about our ideas, we imagine that people wouldn't pay attention. So we do the same thing the economists do. If we look up a word in the dictionary, we call it 'research.' If we try to decide where and how we will spend our money, we call it 'maintaining a budget.' It's not necessary, but we somehow feel more important when we do it."

"Papa, teach me economics."

My heart went to her and I adored her that moment. How often an appeal for knowledge is shunted aside by busy parents. Or guardians.

"I can try, Gigi."

She tossed her dark-brown tresses and her eyes snapped fire. "I guess you think I'm too dumb. You just don't want to."

I looked at her helplessly and she read my surrender.

"Of course I want to. Truly. Now, where will I begin?" I thought for a moment. "Let's start like this. You and I and all the people of the human race live on this one planet."

"Maybe not, Papa. Maybe there are people on other planets, too."

"That is possible. We don't know. There are so many things we don't know. But for our purposes, Virginia, let's limit our discussion to the areas we do know something about. Since nearly all of us will spend all our lives on this one planet, that is what really concerns us. At the present time, instead of letting our imaginations run free as to what life might be like on other planets, we have to confine ourselves to taking a good look at this one.

"You see, if we worry about things beyond our grasp right now, we might forget to deal successfully with our immediate problems. And then we'd forget to plant the corn and raise the cows and chickens and make the plows and till the fields and do the harvesting, and all the other things that have to be done if we are to stay alive here and now. And that's what economics is really about. It's about the here and the now. When we have mastered that, then we'll have time to let our imaginations run free. Do you understand that?"

She nodded. "Like who will get dinner ready if we all dream about Mars and Venus?"

"That's right. Now, let's take a look at this world we're on. Man is a living creature who basically lives on land. We've managed to conquer the air and water and even outer space to some degree. But we are land-based creatures. Sooner or later, we have to put our feet down on dry land."

She nodded. "That makes sense."

"Splendid. Now it happens that this earth is about thirty per cent above water and the rest of our globe is covered with water. So all human beings need land; they must have the chance to occupy land most of the time. What's the fairest way of going about that?"

"That's easy. Give each person an equal amount of land."

"Wait a minute. That wouldn't be at all fair."

"I don't see why not."

"Consider the nature of the land. Some of it is productive and some isn't. Some of it contains rich deposits of minerals, metals, oil. Other pieces of land are rocky and barren. Some bits of land are deserts. Some are covered with forests. Some are good for raising crops. Some land is near oceans, rivers, or lakes. Some land is far from water. Some places get lots of rain. Some get more snow and ice than they get rain. No two pieces of land are alike. So, if you began by giving each person, say, an acre of land, the man who got an acre in the middle of the Gobi Desert might die of thirst before he reached his property. However, the man who got an acre of land in downtown Los Angeles would do very well, indeed."

"Papa, I don't like that. I think the land should be evenly divided."

"Hon, I know how you feel. But the questions we are dealing with are questions relating to reality. We have to know what the facts are. Now, if I'm wrong about the nature of this planet, say so and show me where I am wrong. It won't do us a bit of good pretending that the earth is different from what it really is. Economic study if it has any merit at all, teaches us to deal with things as they are, not as we imagine they are."

"I can see why it's kind of icky."

"Look at it this way, Virginia. However the earth came

into existence—and we have a great many theories about it, but not a single eyewitness account—the earth is what it is. We can recognize its reality, its true nature, and deal with it fairly successfully. Or we can shut our eyes to reality and act on the basis of wishful thinking. Which method will be better?"

"That's easy, reality."

"I think so, too."

"Why didn't someone tell me these things years ago? I should have been told this when I was a child."

"Didn't your classes in geography help to do this?"

"Well, yes, I guess so. But you make it sound different, somehow."

"In what way?"

"Well, when I learned about geography, it all seemed kind of disconnected. I mean, it didn't relate to me. It would have if I'd been rich or could travel. But it was all about all those other people and places. It was hardly at all about anything to do with me. You're making it sound like it affects me."

"Good. It does."

"Okay. So we can't divide the land up evenly."

"What I said, Virginia, is that if we did, it wouldn't be fair."

"All right." She was unhappy about it.

"Let me point out some other things relating to this same characteristic we find on this earth. The varying usefulness of different pieces of land is matched by the enormous differences we all have as human beings. No two of us are precisely alike. Nor are we living in precisely the same way. In some parts of the earth there are impacted populations. That means that a very great many people live in a few square miles, as they do in our major cities. In other parts of the earth we have a sparse population. In still other places there are practically no people at all. So, just like different pieces of land, people are unequally distributed. How fair would it be to insist on moving all the people around until each one had, say, a single acre of land? Look at it realistically. Would you approve of that?"

"I don't think so."

"Would you want to be moved to your own acre of land

while everyone else was moved to his?"

"I wouldn't like that at all. I don't like people moving me around. I want to move by myself."

"Of course you do. Most other people feel the same way."

"Well, what are we going to do?"

"Before we do anything, we have to learn the nature of reality. When we understand it sufficiently well, then we can decide what to do. Right now, we are learning. That's why education is so important."

"I understand that all right. Go on, Papa."

"All right, now, consider the nature of man. No two of us are exactly alike. Some people have a great deal of ability. You, for example, are way ahead of some people in your class. At the same time there may be one or two who are ahead of you."

"You think I'm kind of dumb, don't you?"

"I don't mean it critically, Virginia. I think you do very well. But some are older than you and have learned more and had more experience. Some are younger and know less. There is no one else in the whole world that is exactly your equal. And that's true for all of us.

"This means that some people have enormous energy and ability. Some have modest amounts. Some have very little. Some are young, some middle-aged, and some quite old. So we have a world where everything is unequal. It always has been that way; it always will be. That means that some will excel. If a race is run, one person among the runners usually wins. Is having someone win a race fair?"

"Sure, if they all start off together."

"Well, that's the idea I'd like to dwell on a bit in the interest of being fair. How fair would a race be if it was guaranteed at the outset that whether you could run fast or slow, everyone would win the prize?"

"That wouldn't be a race at all."

"Well, my dear, that's the way life is. In a sense, it's like a race. You learn all you can and then you do the very best you know how. Among those in the group you are in, some will do better and some will not do as well as you will. But if we let them alone and permit each to do the best he can, and then they are rewarded on the ability they show, isn't that what fair is all about?"

"Sure."

"Very well. What we learn, then, as we begin our study, is that universal disequilibrium obtains in all things. Now, that's a fancy way of saying that everything on earth is unequally divided. People, abilities, land, all natural resources—nothing is equal and it can't be made equal.

"Why, Gigi, if we took all the money in the U.S.A. and divided it up evenly this afternoon, by tomorrow morning it would all be unequally divided again. Some people value money a great deal and would work to get more. Others value it very little. Some are willing and able to work hard. Others aren't. What we have to insist on is fair treatment for everyone, regardless of energy or ability. But we mustn't confuse fair treatment with equal division."

"Oh, I see what you mean."

"Gigi, if you see that, you have learned a very great lesson already."

"Well, my gosh, I see that."

I smiled. "Then, my dear, that's all for now. I want you to think about that and we'll talk about it more, possibly tomorrow. Now, I really do have to get back to my notes."

She skipped to the door and then asked, "Is this what economics is like?"

"Well, we've made a beginning. It's really just simple common sense."

"My teacher says that the trouble with common sense is that it isn't all that common."

I chuckled. "Now, that's a teacher worth having."

Her eyes sparkled and she was gone.

Life was indeed a race. To Virginia, my race was nearly over. I wasn't a big winner, but not a loser, either. How would Virginia have put it? To her, I would be "over the hill." But she hadn't said that. She had said all manner of things that praised me.

Suddenly, I was looking into my own heart. Why did I care so much what she thought of me? Was I secretly hoping that she had meant everything she had said? That it was deserved?

I shook my head in self-disapproval, banished Virginia to outer space, and turned to my neglected notes.

Chapter 2

JOY FROM JUNK

Saturday was one of those enchanting spring days that occur on weekends all too rarely. Standing on the back porch, I inhaled the fresh, warm air, lilac-scented and heady as new wine. I stood a moment, watching a squirrel, coat beginning to lose its bedraggled look, as it zig-zagged across the grass with no discernible objective. Perhaps the squirrel, too, had that sense of springtime rejoicing when the buds burst into view and the leaves on the trees grow large and begin to rustle in the soft air currents.

I turned to re-enter the kitchen only to find my passage blocked by a small girl, an enormous cardboard carton clutched firmly to her chest, struggling to get out. I held the door and let her squeeze past.

"What's all that stuff, Virginia?"

The carton was open at the top and I glimpsed an astonishing array of old rags, sticks, a roll of wallpaper, a broken doll, bits of china, and a cockeyed lampshade.

"Junk. I'm taking it back to the alley so the trash man can get it."

"Good idea."

I watched her lug the box to the rear of the lot and waited for her to return.

"Where did you get all that stuff?"

"I'm cleaning my room. Don't interfere or I'll make you help."

"Don't worry. I won't interfere. But why are you throwing the whole big box full of things away?"

"It's junk."

"If it's junk, what was it doing in your room before you threw it out?"

"It wasn't junk, then." She looked at me defiantly. Her faded blue jeans were rolled up about her ankles. She had on floppy tennis shoes, an oversized man's shirt, one of mine I vaguely recalled, and her hair might have responded favorably to a brush.

"What turned it into junk?"

She swung around and faced me, hands on hips, head tilted to one side. "I take good care of my things, Papa. I'm not being wasteful. I don't think you have any reason to scold me."

"Oh, my dear. I'm so sorry. I wasn't scolding."

She puffed out her cheeks and then exhaled. "Some of the things wore out and some got broken and I just don't like that horrid green skirt any more. So I got rid of them. It's all junk." She waved her arms and marched past me into the house. I followed.

"Gigi. Wait a second."

In an elaborate display of patience she stopped and waited.

"It happens," I said, "that I have some spare time and I thought it might be enriched with another lesson in economics."

"Why didn't you tell me the truth, Papa?"

She was on the defensive. But why?

"What do you mean?"

"You told me that economics was the study of how we manufactured things and how all of us have to use land. Well, I happened to make a new friend at school. And she's a junior. And she's taking economics. And I asked her what it was about. And she told me that it's all about cooking, and keeping accounts and running a household. It's all about saving money and being thrifty and things like that. And then I come home and you start to pick on me because you see me getting rid of some old things. Honestly, Papa!"

"I did tell you the truth, Virginia."

"Do you think Mabel is lying, then? Really, Papa. She's *taking* economics. And you said you weren't an economist. Don't you think she'd know something about it if she's taking it?"

"She's taking *home* economics, Gigi. It's not quite the same. But you're not being fair with me. If you remember, we both looked at the dictionary and I was using the dictionary definition about economics. I did tell you the truth. But I will admit that I'm not entirely satisfied with the dictionary definition. Of course, it's just a handy desk copy and a bigger one would probably have a more complete explanation. So I thought this a good time to make a more complete explanation."

"Then why did you jump all over me just because I'm throwing away some junk?"

"I was trying to get you to think through a very interesting process that relates to economics, Gigi. Come on, let's talk about it. Want to come to my study or the living room, or where?"

"Papa, it happens that I'm busy. I have to clean my room."

"Gigi, we've been good friends. I think we still are. But you're all huffy. You're not giving me a chance. The other day I was busy, too. But you got my full attention. Don't you think that turn about is fair play?"

"If turn about is fair play, why isn't it fair to divide all the land evenly?"

I started to laugh. "Good, I'm glad you remembered that. But do you remember that we also agreed that if a race is to be run, it's a fair race if the contestants start out evenly although some will surely finish ahead of others. You and I are having a bit of competition here. Let's treat each other fairly. That means, each of us has his say. But that doesn't mean that I'm going to take away half of your property or that you're going to take away half of mine. It's not the same thing."

She wavered and the hint of a smile twitched her lips. "What about my room?"

"That question could have two meanings, Gigi. It might mean that you're asking about your spring cleaning. Or it might be that you're asking me to your room for our discussion."

"Oh, no, Papa. You can't come to my room. Not right now. It's a mess. I've got it all torn up and the bed isn't made and it's a scary, hairy berry."

"Come here, Gigi." I held out my arms. "A truce. We're in a race but I wasn't trying to trip you up, honest and truly. So you don't have to try to trip me up. I don't know what your room is like or how much work is involved in fixing it. But let me put it this way. I have some time right now. I have to be away this afternoon. You decide. Do you have the time to talk about economics now and still have time to do your room this afternoon? If not, let's forget it."

She took one of my hands in both her small and somewhat grimy ones. "I'm sorry, Papa. You really are very good to me. I . . . well, I guess I was kind of upset about what Mabel told me."

"I really can't say that I blame you, hon. You must have thought I was pretty far off base. But economics is a very big subject. Let's go to the living room. We can open the door and let the spring breezes blow in as we talk. Come on."

We sat side by side facing the big stone fireplace. It was black and soot-charred but in the bright light streaming in the windows, somehow friendly.

"Perhaps I was being a bit devious asking you about the junk you were throwing out. I wanted you to realize that quite often, something we work hard to get, deteriorates in our own evaluation of it. For example, you mentioned that green skirt. I'm sure you were right in getting rid of it. Yet, at one time you must have liked it. I suspect it cost money to buy."

She looked at me closely. "That's the one thing I was kind of worried about. I thought you'd scold me about it. About throwing it away, I mean. It wasn't worn out or torn or anything. It's just that it's yukky. I wouldn't wear it again for anything. I really don't care if it cost quite a few dollars. I don't like it."

"Hon, please. I'm not challenging that. Believe me. We all do that sort of thing. So, in addition to being upset about Mabel, you had a sense of guilt about getting rid of the skirt."

She nodded and one of her hands stole into mine.

"And I made it worse. I'm sorry. I should have let you know that my question was an academic one and not aimed at reprimanding you. Do you think I really care what you do with your skirt, as long as you're happy?"

"I guess not. But it did cost money."

"Right. And perhaps, instead of throwing it out, it might have been wiser to give it to someone else if it's in good shape. Or, perhaps you could sell it. I'm not advising it. I wanted you to see that you and I and everyone else in the world has a very interesting evaluation system. We all function here the same way. We will value things, *more* or *less*. Our values move around. Sometimes we will work hard to get something because we really want it. Other things, which other people may value highly, we wouldn't even have in the house. Isn't that true?"

"You mean it's not wrong?"

"It's neither right nor wrong. It's the way we function. In fact, if you ask your friend, Mabel, about that skirt, I think she'll tell you that in her home ec class she'd be advised to sell the skirt or to give it to a worthy charity or to a friend. But I'm not concerned with home ec. I'm concerned with the underlying principles that affect all economic actions."

"I never thought about selling it or giving it away."

"Of course you didn't. You thought that since *you* didn't like it, it was no good."

"Yes, that's true."

"It didn't occur to you that someone else might think it lovely, even if you think it's . . . er, yukky?"

"Excuse me." Virginia leaped to her feet and dashed from the room. In moments she returned, trailing a bedraggled piece of green polyester.

"I got this out of the trash," she said happily. "I'm going to take it to school and see if anyone wants it. 'Course, I'll have to wash it. It's all rumpled."

"How will you find out which of the girls wants it the most?"

She looked at me, puzzled. "What do you mean, Papa?"

"Well, Gigi, if you take it to school all fresh and looking its best, several girls may want it. Which girl will you give it to?"

"Golly, I don't know. I guess the girl I like best. Maybe Mabel will like it." Her eyes sparkled hopefully. "She's just my size."

"Let's be careful here. Do you want to make a public announcement, letting some of your friends know that you really like someone more than others?"

"I could give it to the girl who likes it who is the poorest."

"True. But how do you know that for sure? Some who are poor are very proud and never let anyone know how really desperate their plight is. Others make their poverty a matter of common knowledge and common complaint. How do you really know?"

She tossed the skirt to the end of the sofa in exasperation. "Papa, you're making it terribly difficult. I really don't know what to do. I'm not supposed to throw it out, but if I give it away I could just cause trouble."

"You might have an auction and let it go to the highest bidder."

"I don't think that would be fair. What about a poor girl who really wants it and doesn't have any money?"

"Let me assure you, hon, that this problem of distributing goods fairly has caused plenty of headaches for some very smart people. So, let me try to help you in this case.

"I'm going to suggest that you put the skirt up for auction to the highest bidder. But instead of making the bids public, have the girls who want and like the skirt give you sealed bids. Have them write down their offers and present them in sealed envelopes. Some may not have any money but might be willing to lend you something of theirs that you like. Or even give you something. Others might have money. Some might want to do you a favor. And then, with no one knowing what anyone else bid, you would be at liberty to accept the bid you liked best. It might be money, or anything else you like. That way, you really give the skirt to the girl you like best if she indicated she wanted it, because no one would know what anyone bid except you."

"Papa, that sounds kind of sneaky. Isn't it dishonest?"

"Not at all. Gigi, every human being is entitled to privacy. Just as it's really nobody's business but your own as to which of your girl friends you like the most, it's none of their business as to what you do with your own property. You have a right to throw that skirt away and if you wish, do so. Or you have a right to give it to someone or to sell it to anyone you choose. It's your skirt. You decide.

"An alternative suggestion would be to just quietly present the skirt to someone you like. But your problem here is that since you don't like the skirt, you might presume that no one would like it. So when you have something you don't like, and you want to find out if others share your view, offer it to the highest bidder and keep to yourself the information you obtain by this method. It's a perfectly sound and practical way to proceed."

Virginia sat quietly, holding her hands tightly together. "I see what you mean. It seems kind of contrary to a lot of other things I've been learning. If I just give it to a girl who I think is poor, she might hate the skirt and throw it away. If that was to happen, I ought to throw it away myself and spare her the trouble. She might accept it because she'd be too polite to turn it down. But she'd hate it and she'd probably hate me, too."

"Very good, Gigi."

"But if I find out who really wants the skirt the most, I could select the girl who wanted it most and who was also poor. And no one would have to know that her bid was low and I just wanted to be generous and help her."

"That's right. Now, if you were in business and were selling skirts for a living, you'd try to have no favorites at all. So you would let the dress go to the highest bidder without fear or favor. And that way you would know that you were being the fairest you could be. It's like running a race, you see. The girl who really loves the skirt and really wants it, will just bid more for it than others. And why shouldn't she have it, since she demonstrates that she wants it more than anyone else? You would bestow the prize on the winner of the race."

Virginia nodded and looked at me, her brown eyes filled with comprehension. "Oh, my. I believe I really do see that. It's a little scary."

"Virginia, I'm very happy that you have demonstrated a basic kindness and concern for those who may be less fortunate. And you have decided to practice sound economics with an item in scarce supply. That is excellent and it takes me to the real point I wanted to make. It means that someone will have a benefit that otherwise could not have been possible. The trash man probably doesn't have time to go through the junk you threw out. So, he'd treat the skirt like a rag and it would ultimately be reprocessed or recycled and maybe end up as paper, or possibly it would even be burned. Your decision to dispose of the skirt in such a way that someone else benefits is excellent. Remember. Only one girl can receive the skirt. You make any selection you wish based on your own scale of values. You can't help everyone. But you can help someone. You decide which one, any way you care to."

She nodded. "I'm beginning to feel like an official judge."

"That's what you are, my dear. Owning and disposing of property is a very responsible process. Be fair. Be honest. And be kind."

"Oh, Papa. That sounds so really good."

"It is good."

"Is that the lesson?"

"Actually, I want to make another point which ties right into this one. What I didn't like about the dictionary definition we read the other day is this. In pointing out that economics is the study of the conditions and laws affecting the production, distribution, and consumption of wealth, the dictionary failed to mention that all economic goods are scarce. As we saw the other day, all resources and all humans and all human abilities are unequally distributed. But additionally, all economic goods are scarce. There aren't enough of them to go around."

"Papa, at school the kids say that there's enough of everything except that rich people have more than they need and the poor don't have enough. But if everything was equally divided, then everything would be all right."

"I realize that many people think that way. But I want you to know the truth, Gigi. And we've already noted the lack of equal distribution in land, resources, and humans. Now I want you to understand what is meant by a *scarce* resource.

"Let's look at it this way. Suppose you were a very rich little girl and had millions and millions of dollars. Would you be willing to go out and work to get more money? If you had so much money that you couldn't even imagine running out of money, how hard would you work to get more?"

She clapped her hands and squealed with delight. "Oh, if only that was true! Of course I wouldn't work to get more money if I had all the money I'd ever want. That would be silly!"

"Suppose you had all the dresses and skirts you'd ever want and even if you ran out of some particular thing, it would magically be supplied. How hard would you work to provide those things?"

"Papa, you're teasing. I don't have things like that." She shook her head and sighed. "I don't suppose I ever will, either."

"True enough. None of us ever has everything we want because everything we want is scarce. Not only are all resources unequally divided, they are in scarce supply, at least under certain conditions. Now, this is very important. Let's see if I can make it clear.

"Way back in the early days when people were trying to figure out what happened when food, clothing, and shelters were produced and distributed, the scholars discovered that people would not spend money or do any work to get things they already had plenty of. So these early scholars decided to call things that were scarce 'economic goods.' Anything in abundance, so plentiful that no one would be willing to spend money for it or would be willing to work to produce it, would be classed as 'non-economic goods.' So, what we are really concerned about are *economic goods*—things that are in scarce supply.

"Now at the outset, the scholars figured that air and water, two of the most important things in the world, are so plentiful that no one would ever work to provide them. Therefore, they at first thought air and water should be classed as non-economic goods.

"But they very quickly found they were wrong. Take water, for example. A man who decided to cross the desert was quite willing to pay money to get a supply of water and a supply of containers to keep the water in as he traveled over the burning sands. Reason? Water is scarce in deserts; sometimes non-existent. Therefore, he valued water high enough *in that situation* to be willing to spend money and to work hard to get a supply of water.

"Of course, if a man is standing beside a freely running

stream, bubbling up out of the earth, and you asked him to give you a dollar for a canteen of water, he'd laugh in your face. *He* has all the water right at his feet that he could ever use. He only has to bend down and dip it out. To *him*, water is a non-economic good. But to the man in the desert, water is an economic good. So he might very well be willing to pay a good price, even for an ordinary thing like water."

"Oh. Sure. I can see that. Wow! I know I would if I was thirsty."

"Of course. And they found the same thing was true if you went to sea. There's plenty of water in the sea. But it's not good drinking water. So, when you sail, you have to spend time and money and energy to make certain that drinking water is provided or you'll die of thirst. Under certain circumstances, water is an economic good."

"Anyone can see that."

"Good. Now, the same is true of air. Most of us don't think about it. We breathe all the time and presume that there will always be an adequate supply of air. But suppose we climb a high mountain. A very high mountain. It may be wise to pack along some small tanks of oxygen for use at high altitudes. The air is thin and in scarce supply up there. And surely we know that if we fly in an airplane or travel out in space, we had best put in some very expensive equipment to provide air *under those conditions*, or we'll stop breathing very quickly. So, many men had to put up the money and spend a lot of time inventing machines and storage tanks that would produce and store supplies of oxygen and just plain old breathing-air, or jet flights and space travel would be impossible."

She nodded vigorously. "Nobody wants to stop breathing."

"So, as it turns out, Gigi, even air and water are in scarce supply under certain conditions. And therefore, under those conditions, air and water are economic goods and we will work hard and spend money to have air and water supplied to us.

"There's another thing. We are beginning to find that a great deal of the breathable air we have gets full of pollutants of one kind or another. This has always been true. Every odor is an air polluter. Billions of plants give off pollen and types of spores which we breathe into our lungs. Some of these cause allergies in certain people. And today, manufacturing, heating, and even automobiles put still other types of things into the air. Fresh breathable air may become a major business in the future. We may, in due course, find it wise to build huge plastic domes over our cities or over our homes so that fresh, breathable air can be produced and made available to us. We don't know. Maybe we can clean up the air sufficiently so that won't be necessary. But maybe not. What I'm trying to point out is that even the air is an economic good under certain circumstances. And the more scarce good, breathable air becomes, the more willing we will be to devote ourselves to hard work and the creation of devices and machines that will supply this vital item. In other words, Virginia, we value things in relation to their scarcity."

Her eyes were big. "I never heard of that before, Papa. Could plastic domes be built over houses and things like that?"

"Certainly. Even over farm land where crops are raised. Few things are as important to good health as clean fresh air. Like the clean fresh air that is blowing into this room right now, thanks to the open door. In fact, I did a little work to make certain that we'd have some good breathable air while we sat here. I opened the door. The expenditure of energy in the accomplishment of a desired goal is called 'work.' " I laughed. "I didn't work very hard, it's true. But I did work hard to pay for the door and get it installed."

"The kids at school say that air pollution is caused by the automobile and that we ought to pass a law against them."

"What would happen if that occurred, Gigi?"

"Well, we wouldn't be able to drive a car any more."

"And what would that mean?"

"We couldn't go for a drive tomorrow."

"More than that. I wouldn't have a job. I depend on my car, in order to work. Now think. At least a million people who make cars and another million who service them and provide the gasoline and other things required would have no jobs. And then the many millions who use cars at their work would all be thrown out of work.

"Now, if I didn't have a job, I wouldn't take in any money. And if I didn't have any money, I would be unable to buy you a skirt, or food, or pay for the lights and gas and other things we have and enjoy."

"Papa, that happens all the time. When people don't buy cars, they stop making them."

"Right. And that effect spreads through all the areas of business, industry, commerce, and finance."

"I guess we'd better not pass a law to prevent cars."

"I guess we better not. Of course, there's nothing wrong with improving cars. They can stand a lot of improvement, in fact. But we surely do need them. Just as we need the food that some people produce, because it is scarce, and the clothing which is scarce. . . . "

"Like my green skirt."

"Correct. There aren't enough skirts to go around, Virginia. So your decision to help meet that scarcity is a good one."

She laughed. "That's funny. Skirts do go around, Papa."

"You know what I mean, hon. And that's the point I really wanted to make. Not only is everything unequally divided in this world, everything that is wanted is in scarce supply."

"I know something that isn't."

"What?"

"Sand. We've got deserts and deserts full of sand. Nobody wants sand."

"Think again, Gigi. Millions and millions of dollars are spent every year by people who buy sand."

She was astonished. "I can't imagine why."

"How do we make cement and concrete? One of the most important ingredients is sand. Not just any old sand, but certain kinds and types of sand. So hundreds of men are hired to deal with this problem. Big machines are produced and trucks are purchased so that sand can be dug up and hauled away to places where roads are being built and buildings are being constructed and so on. Even sand is in scarce supply under certain conditions."

"Oh, my goodness. That's so. I forgot."

"So, Gigi, if even air, water, and sand are in scarce

supply under certain circumstances, then even those things are economic goods. And certainly other things not nearly as plentiful are, too. We'll work hard and spend money to get them because there isn't enough of these things in certain places and under certain circumstances. And that's what economics is about. It's about the production, distribution, and consumption of *scarce resources*. There isn't enough of anything that is valuable. We want the things we don't have enough of. That's what this study is all about."

"Like my skirt."

"Like your skirt."

"Papa, this is a very important thing, isn't it? I mean economics."

"It really is, Gigi. It's basic."

"I know something else that's scarce and very valuable."

"What?"

She squealed in delight. "I'm going to make you guess." She jumped up, then suddenly turned and threw her arms around my neck giving me a powerful hug.

"That's my lesson, isn't it?"

I nodded.

"Then I'm going to give you a lesson, Papa. I'm going to show you how spic and span I can make my room."

She started to leave, remembered, and turned back, snatching up the skirt. Then she marched away in triumph.

All at once the living room was barren and uninviting. I closed the door and went to my study.

What did she mean, she was going to make me guess about something scarce and valuable? She couldn't mean cleaning her room. She wasn't that untidy as a rule.

I could still feel the pressure of her arms about my neck. Virginia was fond of me. I was grateful for that spontaneous expression of affection. I had been preachy, drilling home a lesson, making certain she grasped the fine points. I could have anticipated alienation, boredom. But I was sure she wouldn't have given me that hug unless she had really felt like doing so. She must find me likable to some degree.

Ah, youth. It is so spontaneous and so sincere.

I caught myself with a vacant grin on my face and wiped it off.

Chapter 3

SELFISHNESS — GOOD OR BAD

"Let's go to the beach, Gigi."

Virginia shook her head. "It's too cold, Papa. I don't want to swim."

"Who said anything about swimming? I think it would be fun to go to the beach."

"Do I have to wear my suit?"

"Of course not. Come as you are. In case you decide to go in, you might take your suit. You could change in the car."

"Are you going to swim?"

"No. I just want to get out and see what people are doing at the beach."

She tilted her head to one side in a way that said as clearly as words, "There's no sense in going to the beach but I suppose we women must humor our men." Out loud she said, "Don't you *know* what people are doing? I do."

"Oh, come on," I said. "Don't be an old stick-in-the-mud."

We drove to Santa Monica, turned north, and finally found a parking place. The sparkling crisp weather had produced a horde of sun worshipers and along the sandy strand below us, a motley crowd, in various stages of near nudity, disported themselves in crowds, clusters, and pairs. An occasional beach umbrella added a touch of comfort to the scene. At one end of the beach a volleyball net sagged between two makeshift poles and two groups of teenagers batted the ball back and forth with slight regard for the rules of the game.

As far as the eye could see, sun sparkled on shimmering water. A flock of gulls circled lazily, riding the warming air amid raucous calls.

"It's beautiful, isn't it, Gigi?"

She got out of the car on her side and came to stand beside me. "I think it's hideous."

"You do? Why?"

"Oh, the beach and the ocean are lovely. And it's a beautiful day. And I like those gulls. But, Papa! All those people!"

We trudged across yielding sand and finally found a vacant spot above the high-tide marks. Each wave broke just off the shore and then the sheet of water slid upward across packed sand, pushing a line of foam into place like a fringe of ocean lace.

I sat down, stretching out my legs and resting on my elbows. Virginia sat cross-legged and looked surprisingly athletic in her jeans, blouse, and the brightly colored scarf which helped keep her hair in place against the intimacies of whispering winds.

I let the sunlight rest on my face and then had to squint to see at all. "Hey, this is great. It's good to get out and see what's going on."

"I like being with you, Papa. But I really don't like to be at a place with such a big crowd. Why did you want to come here?"

"Gigi, don't you like people?"

"I guess I like them, all right. But most of them look better with their clothes on."

I laughed. "Hmmm. There goes all those ideas I've been cherishing about young people all yearning to be nudists."

"I don't want to be a nudist."

"I won't insist on it."

"Papa, I think it's ugly."

"Why, Gigi?"

"Well . . . my gosh, look." Her eyes indicated a portly male, round-faced and spindle-legged, who trudged in our direction. He was lobster red above his khaki-colored trunks and his legs were as furry as his head was sparsely covered. His belly was shaped like the oval cover of a giant tureen; had its navel protruded, one could imagine lifting it to find plenty of space beneath for a twelve-pound turkey.

"Do you think that's a pretty sight?" She shuddered.

"He's beautiful, Virginia."

"Papa!" She stared at me in disbelief. "You've got to be teasing!"

"No, Gigi. I mean it. Here's why we look at him differently. In your mind I suspect you are comparing him to a young athlete, molded along the lines of the classical Apollo. And he certainly is no Apollo. You are looking at him with the eye of a critic, comparing him to a preconceived ideal of what you think he ought to look like.

"But I am not comparing him to anything. I recognize his complete individuality. There is no one in the world exactly like him."

"Well, thank goodness for that!"

"Hon, you are being intolerant. And your judgment escapes the real man. Take a look at his face the next time he glances this way. He is a kindly man; a good man. And he has had his problems. He is, perhaps, something of a compulsive eater. But why, Gigi? How has he faced life's problems? What pressures have been put upon him and how has he met them? Naturally, I don't know anything about him. But although he is human and perhaps, like all of us, has made mistakes in judgment from time to time, he is a man who wishes the good. And if we knew more about him, Gigi, I think we would discover that he has performed many kindly acts; has a deep concern and love for those near him; and is probably generous to a fault. In fact, I suspect that generosity is his major problem."

"How could generosity be a problem?"

"Nearly all human beings are very generous or would like to be. Do you know why, Gigi? Let me tip you off to a little secret. Most of us are generous because we like ourselves more that way than when we act differently. So we are generous because it makes us feel good. I suspect he has given away more than was wise or prudent.

"Now, that man has courage. I suspect that he is the proprietor, or possibly an employee, at a garage or filling station. He hasn't made much of a mark on the world. But he is sober, honest, hard-working, and I wager his good deeds far outweigh whatever evil he may have done."

"Papa!" She stared at me open-mouthed. "You don't know anything about him. Maybe he's a banker or a minister or a college professor. What makes you think he's a mechanic?"

"Look at his hands, Gigi. Often, you can tell a great deal by a person's hands. Your eyes are sharper than mine but I believe that's grease imbedded around and under his nails. Of course, it could be paint and he could be an artist. But his hands are not the kind of hands I would expect on an artist. He's a man who uses his hands in his work. He's practical, pragmatic. . . and if you could see what's inside, he's a beautiful person."

She looked closely as the object of our discussion passed just below, between us and the curling waves. She sighed. "You are a very wonderful person, Papa."

"Why do you say that, Gigi?"

"Because you are." She looked into my face with a saucy gleam in her eyes. "I know what he is. He's the mechanic who drives a get-away car for bank robbers. He's a crook. And you can't prove that he isn't!" She laughed merrily.

"Should we ask him?"

"Oh, my goodness, no!"

"Of course you may be right," I conceded. "But the odds are on my side. How many people in the greater Los Angeles area are bank robbers who hire a mechanic to drive their get-away car? Don't tell me. I don't know, either. But how many filling stations and garages are in this same area? Actually, I suspect he's a tourist who has come here from somewhere back east. A man of his age who works in this area probably wouldn't have been quite so eager to pick up all the sunlight he has absorbed. But one way or another—tourist, visitor, or local Angeleno—the odds are on my side. I'd say they are in my favor by better than ten thousand to one."

"That doesn't prove anything."

"Right. I agree. He could be the exception. But now I'll tell you something that may shock you. Even if he is a gangster, he could also be a beautiful person."

"Papa. I don't know what you mean. How can a criminal be a beautiful person?"

"This is a very important distinction, Gigi, and I hope you can see what I mean. Obviously, a criminal act is a vicious act. I do not approve of theft in any degree at all. I'm sure you know that. I do not approve of violence inflicted by one person upon another. And an act of theft, even one performed by stealth, is nonetheless an act of violence. It violates the sanctity of privacy and the earnings and savings of other people against their wills. I totally disapprove. But you know that.

"In the course of my lifetime I have met and talked to many people called criminals. Most of them, in their daily lives, behave quite well. Oh, there are some who go on a rampage and perform a whole series of despicable acts. That is true. And I must concede that once in awhile we find someone who is so ignorant about economic matters that he imagines the system we have is designed to injure him. So he becomes angry at just about everything and spends his time trying to take vengeance against 'society' or those parts of it he believes have wronged him or others. But do you know why? Because he convinces himself that by destroying the system and by injuring those responsible for it, he is doing good. Did you know that?"

"Papa, he can't believe he is doing good by hurting others?"

"It's strange, isn't it, Gigi? But it's true. Every human being acts in terms of what I will call 'plus factors.' He can't help it. All of us act that way. Let me try to explain it this way.

"Man is a sensitive, intelligent animal. And he is an active creature. What I mean is this. Man moves around. He is ambulatory. He has to do things. Man can't survive by sitting in one place and letting nature provide for him. A tree, a bush, and various botanical forms of life behave that way. But not man. A man can't put his feet in the soil, raise his arms to the skies, and expect the sun and rain and the fertility of the soil to nurture him.

"So man is born with drives, compulsions, desires. He *wants*. Man is a *wanting* animal. The result is that man's survival depends upon his ability to obtain certain things which he must have. Food, clothing, shelter, and comforts of various sorts are material things we must all have if we are to survive in this material world in which we live.

"Further, man's first task is to look after himself. And this is one of our problems. We are so sensitive and so intelligent and so generous that we recognize that other people have to have the same things we must have. So, while we help ourselves, we also want to help other people.

"Please understand. The other day I told you how happy I was that you wanted to be generous about your skirt. That *is* good. I admire people who wish to help others. But the only person capable of helping another is one who has successfully learned to take care of himself. You can't give away something you don't have. So if people want to give away food, they must first have the food they propose to give away. If they want to give away money, they have to first have it before they can give it away. Each individual has to put himself first.

"So, Gigi, it works like this. You have to eat. You have to wear clothes. You have to have a shelter of some kind. And there are certain comforts and conveniences you want and must have.

"Now, the proper person to look after you, is you. It may be psychologically gratifying to feed others, but you can't survive on that. You have to have your own food. You have to begin by being selfish. By wanting things for yourself. It is splendid of you to want to help another girl have a skirt. But you can't prevent your own nudity that way. You must first clothe yourself. You must first provide your own shelter, your own comforts. *After that,* it is very rewarding to help others.

"In a sense, it's the same with ideas. Lots of people would enjoy passing ideas along to others. Most of us would like to be admired as fonts of wisdom. But you can't give or share an idea with another until you first have it yourself. Life begins with *you*. So you have to begin by being selfish."

"Papa, at school we are taught that selfishness is bad."

"There are two kinds of selfish. There is the kind of person who knows that he must take care of himself and so goes out to produce the things or the money by means of which he can take care of himself. And this is good selfish. If you don't learn to take care of yourself, you will either be a burden on other people or, in the final analysis, you will die. So being selfish to look after yourself by productive effort is a very good thing.

"There is also bad selfish. This is the kind of selfishness that a person called a criminal displays. He, too, wants to look after himself. But he imagines that he can take care of his own wants best by taking things away from others or by hurting them. Good selfish is when you work and produce to look after yourself. Bad selfish is when you impose on others and take away from them in order to benefit at their expense.

"To look after yourself first is really a great charity. For if you don't keep yourself off the relief rolls or out of the bread line, then you'll become a burden on others. And that is bad selfishness."

"Papa, that is so very clear. I wish someone had said that to me before. Golly. I can see that. But I still don't see why you would say that a criminal could still be a beautiful person."

"It's a funny thing, Gigi. A man will live many years and harm no one. He will be productive and take care of himself. And then, perhaps pressures become so great he can't seem to stand up to them; or, most probably, he doesn't understand how an economy really works, and then he'll take a shortcut one day and steal something from someone. It happens a very great deal of the time.

"If that man is discovered at the time he commits a wrongful act—and keep in mind, Gigi, any act of theft is a wrongful act—we brand him a criminal. We overlook all the good he may have done. We dismiss his hard work, his good and constructive efforts. We suddenly find that he did something he shouldn't have done. And now he is no longer human, in our eyes. He's a *criminal.* And we imagine that from that time on, every act he performs will be criminal."

"But won't it be, Papa?"

"No. Criminal actions are always numerically marginal. That means that considering the total number of people alive, only a very few criminal actions take place. We couldn't survive as a species if every man who once stole something continued to steal at every turn. For example, I was a thief at one time in my life. When I was nine, I went with some other boys into my neighbor's orchard and stole apples. That was an act of theft. Fortunately for me, I wasn't caught. Had I been caught, I might have been branded a criminal. And from that time on, everyone would have looked at me as a potential wrongdoer. And it wouldn't have been true."

Virginia thought about that and got very still.

I sensed that I had made a point that had ramifications beyond what I had intended.

Suddenly she leaned forward and laid her hand softly on my chest.

"Papa, I'm a thief."

"I doubt it. Why do you say that?"

"Because I stole."

"Did you? What did you take?"

She extended a leg and plunged her hand into a pocket and pulled it out, her fist tightly closed. There were tears in her eyes.

I sat up straight. "What is it, Gigi?"

Slowly her fingers lifted from her palm. A ring I had given to my wife years earlier sparkled in the sunlight.

"Why did you take that, Gigi?"

"Well, she doesn't wear it, and it is so beautiful, and I wanted it and so I took it."

"You are right, Gigi. That was an act of theft."

"Here." She thrust it at me.

I shook my head. "I don't want it."

"Don't you want to give it back to her?"

"No."

"Do you want me to keep it?"

"What do you want to do with it, Gigi?"

"I want you to take it back."

"To the best of my ability, Gigi, I refuse to be a receiver of stolen goods. You are the one who took the ring. You have to figure out what to do with it. I won't take it off your hands."

"But I'm a thief, aren't I?"

"No. You are a young lady named Virginia. And you're a beautiful person. You did steal something. And the act was wrong. The act was not beautiful at all. I cannot approve of the act. But I still love you and believe in you and know that you will do the right thing."

"Papa, I can't go to Loy and give it back to her. I just can't."

"Why not?"

Tears were coming. "She's been so good to me. And she'll hate me. And I really love her a lot! Oh, dear, what can I do?"

"You can think about it and decide what you want to do."

She stared into the distance. "When I took it, I thought I'd keep it until I got older and then . . . maybe I'd get to go to a dance or a party or something and I'd wear it then and sort of let everyone think it was mine."

"I take it you don't want to do that any more."

"Oh, Papa, I've been bad. I've been terribly, terribly bad." She sobbed and her words choked out between moans and cries. "Oh, I'm a thief! I'm a terrible person. What can I do? Oh, I wish I was dead!"

"Gigi. Listen to me carefully. You are not a thief. You are right now showing just how fine and beautiful a person you really are. Actually, this is the very point I wanted to make. You perform thousands of non-criminal actions every day. You are not a thief. But you did make a mistake, and it is a serious one. I won't relieve you of your responsibility. You have to solve this problem all by yourself."

"I hate this old ring." She was getting control of herself.

"It's the same ring it was when you took it. And it's just as beautiful now as then."

"I could throw it away."

"But you didn't throw away your skirt. You are making arrangements so someone else will have the benefit."

She brightened. "Does that mean that I ought to sell the ring or give it to someone I like?"

"The skirt and the ring aren't quite in the same situation, are they, Gigi? The skirt was yours to keep, destroy, give away, or sell. But the ring belonged to Loy. Before you dispose of it, you might like to ask her about it. It would be up to her to give it away or sell it, keep it, or destroy it, I should think."

"I know! I could tell Loy that I borrowed it."

"You could. But it wouldn't be true, would it?"

"I can't just tell her I'm a thief. What will she think?"

"What will she think if you don't tell her?"

"She doesn't even know I took it."

"Sooner or later, she'll miss it. And what then? Whom do you want to blame for your action? Do you want to tell her I took it? Or that someone else did?"

"Oh, Papa." She was going to cry again. "You're not helping me a bit."

"That's right. You have to be selfish. You have to look after yourself. Do the selfish thing."

"Why, Papa! That would mean that I should keep the ring!"

"No, Gigi. I'm suggesting that you examine your values. Which is more important? Having the ring or being fair?"

"I guess I ought to be fair."

"Gigi, you are now seeing just how bad a society of even three people would be if everyone stole. Let's suppose that Loy and I begin to steal things. Where would that put you? We'd take things away from you and then when you found them missing, how would you manage if we insisted that someone else had taken them? You'd know better. People always know. Presently, no one of us would trust each other at all."

She sighed. "All right." She looked at the ring again. "It's awfully pretty, isn't it, Papa?"

"I think so."

"Loy ought to have it back."

"I have to agree."

"She'll never love me again."

"Think that through, Virginia. Think about whether she will love you more if you return the ring or if you don't."

The ring went back into the pocket.

"Can we go, now?"

"Sure."

We trudged back to the car.

Before starting it, I turned to a little girl, who sat very still and as far from me as she could.

"We've learned so many economic lessons today that I want to take a moment to summarize them. First, I've proposed the idea that people everywhere, all people, act in terms of what they view as 'good' at the time they act. You thought it was a 'good idea' when you took Loy's ring. Now you are engaged in re-thinking that experience. Perhaps you exercised bad judgment.

"People act to prevent loss. And to acquire the things they want. Whether they act to prevent a loss or to make a gain, they are acting in terms of plus factors as they see them at the moment.

"When you took the ring, taking it seemed like a plus factor. You will return it to Loy if and when you see that act as a plus factor.

"All people act in terms of plus factors. They can't act any other way. The person we call a criminal is guilty of bad selfishness. But when that person goes to work to produce money or goods or services so that he can have more of what he wants and not lose that which he has, that is good selfishness. Each of us has to take care of himself.

"People are really beautiful in themselves. They may not look beautiful on the outside and many of us don't. We get old and fat or skinny. We have blemishes and all kinds of odd-looking departures from the classical models. An action that is bad-selfish is like a blemish, or a belly that is too fat or maybe like a wrinkle. And all of us have blemishes in our behavior and sooner or later we have them in our appearance. But the person can still be beautiful inside. The real person always seeks the good and just makes incorrect value judgments as to how to achieve that good."

She wouldn't look at me and her chin was trembling.

I found a radio station with some cheerful music and we drove home with very little conversation.

As we drove, I found that I was gnawing my lip. Had I been cruel? I fretted that I had been unnecessarily harsh.

Virginia was so tiny, such a forlorn bundle of woe, that I wanted nothing so much as to comfort her. I was tempted to stop and gather her into my arms. She was such a precious girl. I wanted to protect her from any and all injury.

Yet I had permitted myself to become the backstop against which her own actions bounced and ricocheted. I had been firm. That was the ultimate kindness, wasn't it? Reality rules us all, and reality is often harsh. But why did I have to be on the side of reality? Why couldn't I be on Virginia's side?

I was as miserable as she was. My heart reached out to her. Silently, the words formed that I wanted to use. But I remained mute.

This is true involvement, I said to myself. This is what it is to be a teacher. It is to see and to feel through the eyes of one's student. Yes, even through the heart and mind of the student. And then, with the student to find truth.

And I remembered something Virginia had said to me earlier. She had indicated we could teach each other, taking turns.

I was consciously trying to help her mature. But it was entirely possible that our roles had reversed. She wasn't trying to teach me a thing; yet I was learning truth, too. And the truth was that there was a living bond between us.

Walk very carefully, I said to myself. You hold her heart in your hand, and you could injure her dreadfully.

I stole a glance at that tear-stained face, and then I knew. She held me in her hand and if she clenched her fist, my own heart would bleed.

Chapter 4

PLUS-FACTOR PROFITS

Loy and I were at dinner Tuesday night before Virginia came in from school. I wouldn't have known of her arrival except for the sound of stealthy footsteps in the hall. Then the door to her room closed.

When we had finished eating, I went to Virginia's room and knocked. There was a long pause and then I heard a muffled voice. I interpreted the sound as an invitation and opened the door.

Virginia was seated in her rocking chair, apparently trying to rock as hard as possible. She was gripping the arm rests with knuckles that gleamed white and she stared into nothingness, her face a study of someone who is trying not to think.

"Would you like something to eat, Gigi?" I asked. "Loy and I missed you."

"Leave me alone, Papa."

"Certainly, if you say so. I just wanted to be helpful if there is anything I can do."

"Why do you want to help me?"

I shrugged. "I guess it makes me feel good when I'm useful to someone."

"Are you being selfish when you want to help me?"

"Of course. If I can be of help, it makes me feel important."

She stopped rocking. "You ought to have nothing to do with me, Papa. I'm a rotten person."

"Gigi, if you're still thinking about that ring, you can forget it. Loy told me how sweet you were when you returned it. I was impressed favorably by the way you admitted your mistake."

"She was terrible to me."

"Why, Gigi! Terrible? She told me you got a big kiss and hug for clearing up the mystery and being honest enough to admit your error."

"That's what I mean. She wouldn't punish me, either. And how do you think that made me feel? Honestly, I could have crawled under a rock. She was so *nice*. And so were *you*. And I was so *beastly*! I don't know how you can stand being with me at all!"

"Virginia, did it ever occur to you that both of us were punishing you? We really were, you know. We punished you by letting you continue to be responsible for your actions. If we had railed at you, deprived you of a privilege, or physically imposed on you, you might have said to yourself, 'Fine, I hurt them and now they've hurt me. So we're even.' But instead, we permitted you to think the whole thing through and the punishment you have inflicted on yourself was more severe than any we could have supplied aggressively. Most of us are ruthless with ourselves when we find we've made an error.

"But, Gigi, that's all over and done with. Let's say no more about it. Come on and have your supper."

"I'll never eat again."

I managed to keep a straight face. "I certainly won't force you to eat. But starving is a very lengthy process."

I went to her dresser and picked up a tiny cushion in which she kept pins, needles, and one enormous hat pin.

"If you feel the need of further punishment, why not start sticking pins and needles into yourself? It can be quite painful, I'm told. But at least you can punish yourself more quickly and practically than by the prolonged agony of starvation."

She struggled against it, but a smile was forcing away the overcast.

"Oh, Papa, you say the most impossible things."

"I guess I do."

"I'm not upset about the ring any more. Really. I'm mad at myself for something else."

"Gigi, my sweet girl, you can't go through life being

mad at yourself all the time."

"Oh, yes, I can. I deserve it. I'm a very, very bad, horrible, rotten person."

"Well, you certainly could have fooled me. What have you done that's so terrible this time?"

"I was just plain rotten, that's all."

"Want to tell me about it?"

She shook her head and screwed up her face. Then all at once she blurted, "All right. I'll tell you. And then you'll see what I mean. It's about my skirt. I took it to school all washed and pretty. And I had sealed bids, Papa. Like you told me. And six of the girls liked it and said they wanted it. And they all handed me notes during the day telling me what they would give for it. And there was one girl who is quite poor. And she didn't have anything for me, but just told me how much she wanted it. But there was another girl, one I hardly know at all. And I don't even like her. And she offered me $20.

"Twenty dollars, Papa! For that yukky old skirt! And, Papa, you won't believe this. Because I didn't like her, I sold it to her. I really did. Because I didn't like her, I cheated her! And because I wanted the money. And that's why I'm late. Because I went to the store after school and I shopped and shopped around, and I bought myself a ring with the money. See?"

She held up her hand. I hadn't noticed it before, but she wore a sparkling bit of paste or glass on her middle finger.

"I guess that tells you what kind of a person I really am. You see, I WANTED to give the skirt to the girl who was poor. And I would have, too, except that this other girl I don't like offered me so very much. And I'm such a greedy, selfish person that I took the money and bought the ring. So there!

"And Papa, I don't really feel bad about it. That's the terrible thing. I'm mad at myself for not feeling terrible. I'm really glad I did it. I wanted a ring terribly much."

I took her hand and gazed at the ring. "It's very beautiful, Virginia. You made an excellent choice. It's the very kind of ring I would have wanted to get for you myself if I had wanted to get you a ring."

"Oh, no, it isn't, Papa. It probably looks genuine to you and I could make a lot of people think it was genuine, but it really isn't. You wouldn't get me one like this. If you got me one, it would cost a great many dollars. Don't tell me that isn't true, because I priced them." Her eyes grew big. "Oh, boy, were they expensive! But this one *looks* like a real one and I could afford it so I got it. And I'm glad I did, but I'm mad at myself for being glad."

"I am unable to see anything you tell me as being a reason for unhappiness."

"But Papa, I think it's terrible. That other girl needed the skirt. And I wanted to help her. I really did. But I wanted the ring even more. And that's rotten."

"Hon, if you are going to feel badly every time you look after yourself, you are going to live a miserable life. Do you think I felt guilty when I bought Loy her ring?"

"Oh, that's different."

"In what way? Don't you think there were plenty of people in the world who were poor when I bought the ring? And I'd like to help them, too. But the interesting thing that you did when you bought the ring, and which I did, too, when I bought Loy's, is that each of us helped in a small way from preventing poverty from occurring in a number of places.

"You see, Gigi, it works like this. You paid a few dollars for that ring. Now, where did that money go? It went to pay the wages of the people working in the store where you bought it. That's where most of it went. Some of it went to pay for the manufacture of more rings. So it helped the manufacturers of rings, and the miners of metals and the skilled craftsmen who designed and fabricated that ring. And it went to encourage all kinds of people who are doing all kinds of useful and constructive things. It made it possible for the jeweler to pay for his lights and gas and other overhead. And it may have resulted in a penny or two in a return to him as a reward for his investment. Your money is being constructively used all down the line. Instead of helping one person, you have helped a horde of people!"

She stared at me unwaveringly. Then she frowned. "But I really kind of took advantage of that girl, I mean the one who bought it, didn't I? The skirt isn't worth $20. That's as much as you paid for it when it was new. And it's a second-hand skirt."

"To the girl who bought it, it was worth it. As a matter of fact, right at the time she bid on it, it was worth more to her than $20. I don't know why she wanted the skirt, either. That's her business. But she had the $20 and she didn't have the skirt. And she weighed the value of the skirt against the value of the $20 and she acted selfishly—selfish good. She got what she wanted by giving up something that she wanted less than what she got in return."

"Are you saying that she took advantage of me?"

"No, Gigi. Neither of you took advantage of anyone. In your judgment, you liked the money better than the skirt. Especially that much money. In her judgment, she liked the skirt better than the money. Possibly she has a lot of money and she really wanted that particular skirt."

"Oh, that's true. Her folks are very rich. She always has plenty of money. That's why most of us don't like her."

I laughed. "Come on, hon, that's no reason for liking or not liking a person."

"Papa, I really kind of had the feeling that she bid that much for the skirt because she wanted me to like her. And I didn't like that at all. And I don't like her."

"You may be correct about her intentions, Gigi. Like everyone else, she wants to be liked. And quite possibly, in view of the sealed-bid auction you conducted, she felt that this was her chance to impress you favorably. She could easily get more money. But she wanted the skirt and she wanted you to believe that she wanted you as a friend, too."

"Did she try to buy my friendship?"

"Of course. It's quite likely. We all do this all the time, Gigi. You always try to buy friendship."

"Well, that's terrible. I most certainly do not!"

"Let's see. I believe you said you made a new friend the other day. Her name was Mabel, if I remember correctly."

"That's true. But I didn't offer Mabel some money. Good heavens."

"Of course not. But I'll wager you did your best to let Mabel know that you admired her and would like her as a friend. Perhaps you even offered to do her a favor of some kind."

"Papa, that's weird. How did you know?"

"I didn't *know*, Gigi, but it's quite usual. You see, it's a very selfish thing to want a good friend. So usually, when we find someone we admire and like to be with, we do our best to convince that person of our affection by letting them know in subtle ways that we'd consider it a privilege to be helpful. So, in a sense you are offering something for something. You were showing Mabel just how nice you could be and that it really would be to her advantage to have you as a friend."

Virginia nodded with a solemn expression. "Papa, you make it sound sort of materialistic. But that's just what I did do. I tried to figure out what Mabel might like about me and I figured that one of her problems was pencils. That's how I happened to get acquainted with her, really. We met in the hall and she had lost her pencil and she needed one and didn't have time to get one. Well, I have that lovely box of pencils and things that I've had for years. So I gave her one of my pencils. And she did like that."

"Of course. Quite the proper thing to do."

"But that's not the same as money."

"Why not? The pencil was bought with money. Mabel didn't want money but she needed a pencil. And you made a friend by helping her in a way that she appreciated. That made both of you feel good."

Virginia laughed in delight. "Papa, Mabel really does have a problem with pencils. She's always losing hers. I gave her another one today. But it doesn't seem like the same thing."

"It's just the same, Virginia, when you look at it through the eyes of the praxeologist . . . the person who studies human action in the market."

"Am I a praxe . . . a pra . . . what it was you said?"

"Not yet. But I hope you will become one."

"No, Papa. I just don't agree. It's not the same. A pencil is such a little thing. Twenty dollars is a lot."

"Not true, hon. Think more deeply. To you, the skirt was a little thing, even a yukky thing. But you found out that to six other girls it was a desirable thing and to one of them, a very desirable thing.

"To you, pencils are little things. You always see to it that you have plenty of them. But to Mabel, who loses them, pencils are terribly important. You supplied something that was very scarce so far as she was concerned.

"The girl who bought your skirt gave you something that to her was a little thing. Dollars. She has plenty of dollars, just as you have plenty of pencils. So she helped to supply what she suspected you would value highly, just as you supplied something you figured Mabel would value highly. Your motive and the motive of the girl you don't like were the same. Your medium of exchange differed, but you were both doing the same thing."

"Papa, I can see that! Oh, my. That does make everything look quite different."

"But isn't it true, Gigi? You see, our concern is to find out what the truth really is. We must put aside all preconceived notions and look at the world and at the people in the world as they really are. That's what economics is all about."

"You make it sound as if my taking all that money was perfectly all right."

"Of course it was. And you made the choice. It was a good one. You could have thrown away the skirt but you decided instead to see if anyone could benefit by it. And remember, skirts are in scarce supply. There aren't enough of them to go around. Please, Gigi - I'm not repeating your pun! So you helped to make another girl happy. You could only give the skirt to one girl. And you chose the one who also made you happy by giving you enough money so you could get the ring you wanted.

"That's called a fair exchange because both parties to the exchange made it voluntarily. No one was injured. And when you spent your money, another voluntary action on your part, the money went into the market to reward a great many hard-working people. I think you acted wisely and with kindness all around. My only concern is that you didn't approve of what you were doing."

"But that's it, Papa. I really did want to help that other girl."

"Of course you wanted to. And we'll talk about that

more in detail some other time. Remember, I told you the other day that looking after yourself is the greatest charity. As someone once said, charity begins at home. I don't know that he meant the same thing I do, but looking after yourself certainly prevents you from being an object of charity so far as others are concerned. And that's what learning about economics is all about.

"Now, hon, why don't you scoot in and have a bit of supper? Loy's kept it hot for you. And we'll talk some more about economics in a day or so."

Chapter 5

THE CONSTANT CHANGE

Virginia bounced into my study late Friday afternoon, her face aglow, her eyes flashing.

"Oh, Papa!" she cried, "I'm so glad it's Friday!"

"Great," I agreed. "What's so exciting about this particular Friday?"

"Nothing."

"You look as though you'd stumbled on the diamond mine."

She danced over to me and flung her arms about my neck, giving me a kiss. "I've found a kind of diamond mine."

"Have you really?"

"Sure. You remember I told you the other day that I knew about something that is terribly scarce and terribly valuable and that I'd make you guess what it is?"

"Yes," I said. "But I haven't been able to imagine what you mean. Want to tell me?"

She nodded, the image of potential mischief.

"I'm waiting."

"Can't you guess?"

"Gigi, I'm not a mind reader. I give up."

"It's us," she said happily.

"How do you mean that?"

"Well, it's us. You and me. And Loy of course. It's the relationship we have. It's a very scarce thing. Nearly all the kids at school are always griping about their parents and about how nobody understands them at home. But you and Loy are so good to me. And you do understand me. Both of you. And I'm a very lucky girl. And that's my diamond mine."

"Why, Gigi. . . What a lovely thing to say! Thank you very much."

"It's true, isn't it? You said that things are valuable because they are scarce. And having a good relationship with your parents is very scarce. And I got to thinking about that and I could see I have a very valuable thing."

"Loy and I aren't your real parents, Gigi. You know that. We're just sort of temporary guardians."

"That's what makes it so special. If you were my parents, you'd *have* to love me. At least I think you would. But you and Loy love me and you don't have to. And that's special!"

"You are a most provocative little witch," I said. "And of course we love you. It would take a lot of hard work not to."

"And you forgive me for the terrible way I acted. You do, don't you?"

"Of course, Gigi. And let me congratulate you."

"What for?"

"For beginning to think along economic lines. And that's exactly what you're doing as you recognize the nature of scarce resources—which include friendship and other valuable relations."

"I think economics is exciting. At least it is the way you explain it."

"Thank you. You said that you were glad it's Friday. We had the same relationship Thursday. What makes today so special?"

"It's the last day of school for this week, silly."

"I thought you like school."

"I do. And especially my English teacher. He's a dream. He's kind of scarce, too. So I like him. But my other teachers are kind of plentiful and I don't like them as much."

She joined in my laughter. Then she said, "If you think about it, Papa, you'll see why I have to like weekends better than school. A weekend is only two days long and the school lasts five days. So weekend days are scarcer than school days. So I like them better."

I blinked. "I never thought of it that way. But you're

right, of course."

"Then I'm learning?"

"You most certainly are. Now, get a chair. What I want to show you today will require a chart. If I had a blackboard, I'd use it. But I can draw the model on a piece of paper so we can both look at it."

She crowded her chair next to mine and sat down as I drew a few sheets of typing paper from a drawer.

I drew a line that looked like this:

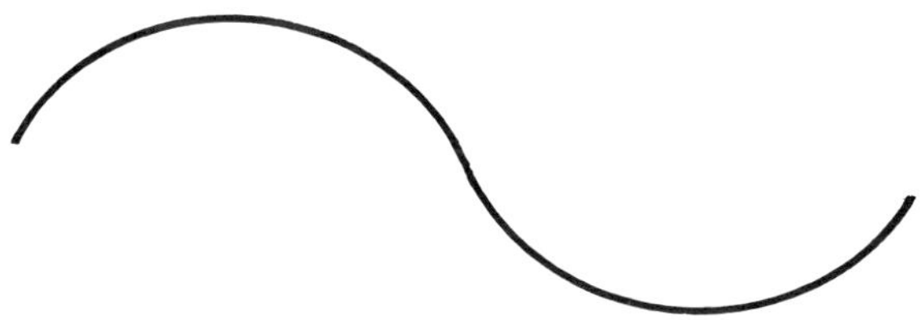

She looked at it doubtfully. "Is that an economic principle? It looks like a scriggly old snake."

"It will illustrate one of the most important laws we know of, Gigi. It's called the law of supply and demand."

"It doesn't make much sense to me yet."

"Let me review for a moment. We discovered that every economic good, including friendship, is in scarce supply. And we also discovered that all resources are unequally distributed. So, while there isn't enough of anything under certain circumstances, what does exist is more plentiful in some places than in others."

"I remember."

"We also learned that human beings act because of plus factors. That is, they value certain things more or less and then act to get or to keep the things they value most. Since everything is scarce, we have to keep on acting to get the things we want and to keep from losing the things we value."

"I remember. Selfishness. Good selfishness and bad selfishness."

"Correct. Now, I've linked a convex and a concave

curve. That's what this 'scriggly old snake' is supposed to illustrate. And you've just been telling me about how it works."

I drew in a minus and a plus sign.

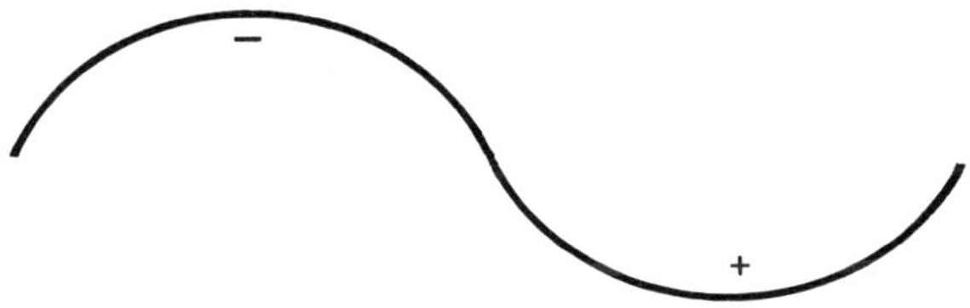

"What this shows is that where one certain kind of goods is plentiful, people tend not to value that particular good. The man standing beside a fresh spring will not value water very highly because to him, the water is plentiful. The man going into the desert will value water very highly because in the desert the water is scarce. So, although we all value water, we value it more or less depending on how much is readily available to us. And that's what this little model indicates. Where we have abundance, as illustrated by the convex curve, negative factors occur. But where there is a scarcity, as shown by the concave curve, plus factors appear.

"What that means, hon, is this. People will pay very little for things they have in abundance. They already have all they want of that particular item. But people may be willing to pay a great deal for something they want that is in very scarce supply."

"Sure. That's easy. I can see that. How very clever to draw it like that. Could I use that drawing to show Mabel?"

"You can make a drawing of your own, but you can certainly use this model. Actually, most economists don't use this explanation because they like to use arithmetic to demonstrate the same point. But you don't like arithmetic and, frankly, I'm not too fond of it myself. You can learn about economics and how things work without relying on arithmetic.

"Most economists begin their explanation with a model that looks like this:

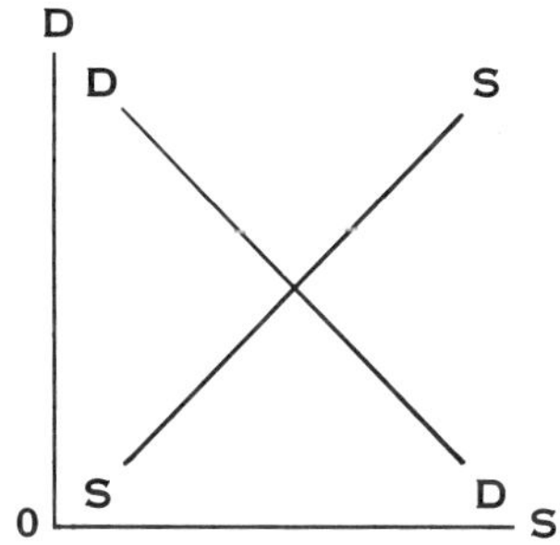

"I've drawn this so the vertical line indicates demand and the horizontal line indicates supply. And the two crossing lines indicate rising and falling demand and supply.

"Now I'm going to put in some hypothetical numbers. If you work it out with figures, you can be very precise about it. But our purpose is to understand how it works and not to solve arithmetic problems. Right?"

She looked at the second drawing. "That's more complicated than the scriggly line and I'm not sure I understand it."

"In this model, the same thing is shown. Start at the corner where I've drawn in a zero, and then put evenly spaced numbers on the horizontal and vertical lines. Like this:

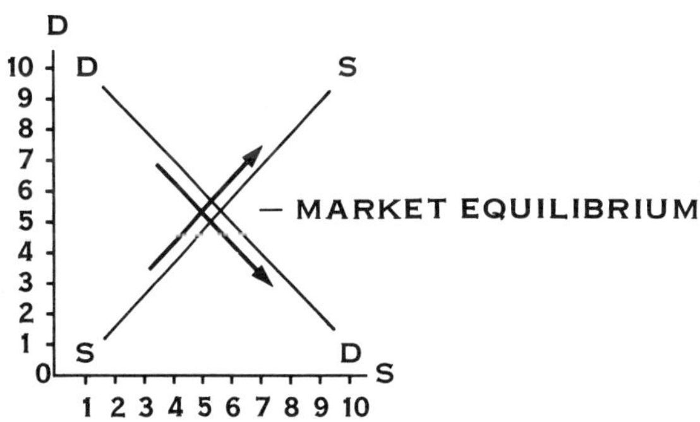

"Now what you see is this. If the supply is low, say only one item in existence, demand will be high. As supplies rise, demand falls proportionately. If supplies become plentiful, demand for the item falls. And the place where the two lines meet in the middle is 'market equilibrium.' You see, you read the chart from left to right and come down on the demand diagonal as you go up on the supply diagonal."

She studied it for a bit. "Yes, I think I see what you mean. But why does it act that way, Papa?"

"This is something that most economists don't like to admit, Gigi, but the law of supply and demand is really a *psychological* law. All economic actions are human actions. And this tells us how human beings will *tend* to act. Always.

"But let's get back to my first drawing because I think we can see a great deal more with it than we can with the mathematical model, although there's nothing wrong with using arithmetic as an aid in understanding. In fact, it's very helpful and it can be done with great precision when it's used.

"A very important point to keep in mind is this. Many people begin to believe that everything happens in the market *automatically*. It doesn't. Nothing happens automatically. Property and things don't make decisions. People do. So nothing will ever be produced or distributed or consumed until some person decides to produce or distribute or consume.

"So, somebody has to make a decision. He has to decide to act. As you did when you took your skirt, which you didn't like, to a place where skirts were in relative short supply. You found out that skirts were in short supply at school. If there had been a complete abundance of skirts, no one would have wanted yours. So you took an item that you had in plentiful supply—seeing that you didn't want it any more—and you took it to a place where you found that a demand existed. And you filled that demand for one person.

"Other girls wanting skirts are going to have to go to the store. In the stores they have an abundance of skirts. They were put there because some people figured that there might be a scarcity of skirts. So they produced an abundance of them in the stores. And those who have a scarcity of skirts go to the store and trade in order to alleviate the scarcity."

"What's alleviate?"

"Sorry. A big word again. It means to ease. The shortage is a little less short because someone eases the shortage by providing goods."

"I see that. Wow."

"Now, if all the women in the Los Angeles area had all the skirts they would ever want, the storekeepers couldn't sell any skirts. But they figure that if they make attractive skirts, women don't have enough of them and thus will come in and buy."

"It's really quite simple, isn't it, Papa?"

"Sure, when you look at it correctly. Now, let's take a look at my first model again.

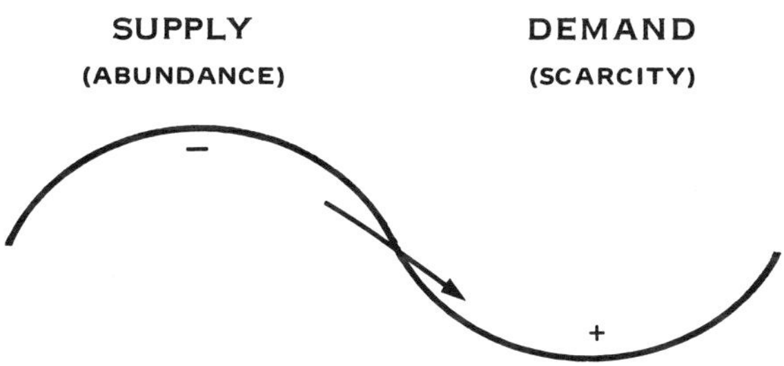

"We also discovered that everyone in the world is seeking a plus factor. And where are plus factors found? *Only* where there are scarcities. See? I'm drawing a diagonal line with an arrowhead at one end. This tells us that people in those places where there is an abundance of a resource will be happy to sell to those in the areas where there is a scarcity. Further, it shows that where there is a scarcity, people will be willing to buy. Some will be happy to sell because to them it will mean a plus factor, a profit. That's why goods and services move from raw materials into factories; from factories into stores; from stores into homes. Each person is seeking a plus factor. Each is acting in terms of his own best interest as he sees it at the time — because each person always seeks that which is best for him at the time, *as he understands it.*"

She clapped her hands. "Then, that means that pretty soon all the minuses will move into the place where all the pluses are and everyone will be happy!"

"It looks that way, Gigi, but that will never happen. Let me show you why."

I drew a line of dashes across the two curves at a median point.

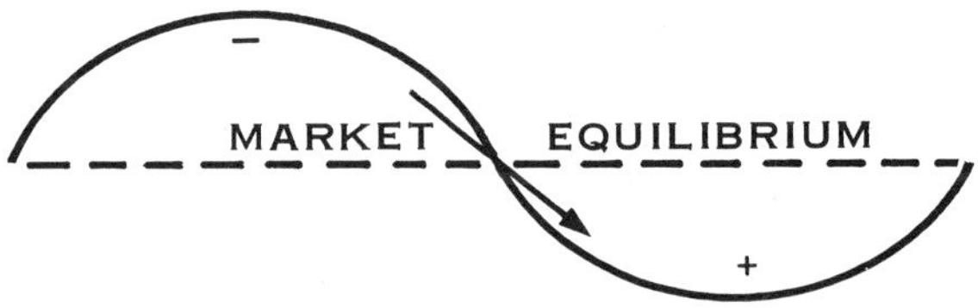

"This line is like the point of intersection on my other model. It's 'market equilibrium.' It means a market in balance or a cleared market.

"Here's what occurs. As producers bring their supplies into the area where there is a demand, supplies dwindle where there are negative factors, and supplies increase where there are plus factors. So this happens next. The producers do such a good job of trying to take care of demand that they overdo it. They always do. They hate it, but they can't help it. And the reason for this is that we cannot predict individual human action. We can only approximate what people will do in groups; never individually.

"For example, your teachers in school can tell you about what is called a 'bell curve.' It looks like this:

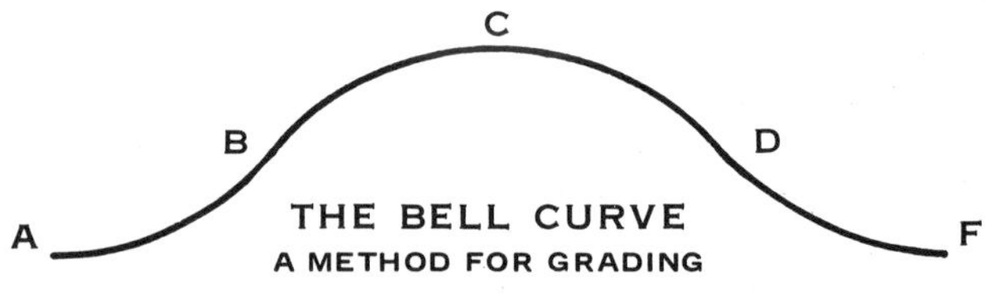

"They can safely predict that if they give a test, a very few will score high and a very few will score low, but most will be in the middle area. That's what a 'C' grade means. It's in the middle. It isn't good and it isn't bad. It's average. And most scoring will show up this way. It's predictable.

But what the teachers can't do, unless they get to know you real well, is predict how *you* will score. In general, all students will score within the bell-curve model, but no one can tell in advance just who will be where.

"Nor can anyone tell when an individual will change his preferences—when his desire for a scarce good will shift to a negative factor. There's a reason for that, too, Gigi. You see, people's values change and shift all the time. Just as yours did. You first wanted the skirt. That's when you got it originally. Then you grew to dislike the skirt. Then you wanted to give it to a certain girl. But you ended selling it to another. Each time you made a decision. And you made it on the basis of your values, as it seemed best to you at the time.

"Everyone does this all the time. We don't value anything absolutely. We value things comparatively. We value money, but not absolutely. If we valued it absolutely, we'd never spend it; we'd keep it forever. But we value it comparatively; relatively. Your customer valued the skirt more than the $20. You valued the $20 more than the skirt. Under other circumstances, you might have looked at it quite differently.

"Since this is what is happening with all people all the time, the men who are in business to produce and make things, do so *hoping* that when they have the goods ready, people will be glad to pay for them. But that isn't always true. People change their minds. Something else looks more important to them, and they stop buying what they had been purchasing and buy something else. So, sooner or later, every businessman has to face this. And so, sooner or later, he does what we call 'over produce.' It looks like this:

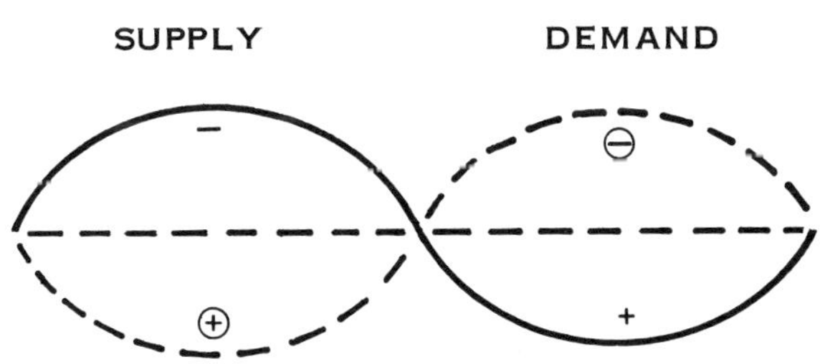

"He delivers so much of a given item to his potential customers that they stop buying. In other words, when supplies rise above the equilibrium level, negative factors appear where before there were only plus factors. And because he ships so much away from where he is doing the producing, the people in that area begin to experience a shortage so it pays him to try to supply the immediate market rather than going elsewhere for customers.

"Thus, supplies and demands never hold still. They shift around all the time. If necessary, he stops producing entirely, for there is no point in producing things that people won't buy. When he does this, people will use up the overage and again the demand will rise."

"I see what that's like."

"Do you?"

"Yes. Remember our trip to the ocean last Sunday? It's like the ocean."

"How do you mean?"

"Well, the ocean is full of waves, but they don't stand still. You know when you watch the ocean that a wave is higher than the trough right next to it. So it will move to fill up that trough. Only, another wave comes along behind it. That's what you mean, isn't it?"

"That's an excellent analogy, Gigi. Very good. Very good, indeed. And just like the ocean, human demands are never still. You'd think that after all these millions of years, the law of gravity would have affected every drop of water in the ocean so at last it would be calm and level. But it never happens.

"Just like human demand, the forces affecting the ocean shift around, too. Not only is gravity acting, but the pull of the moon, the winds, and the heat from the sun and the cold from the Arctic regions. So the ocean is always in motion, dancing, leveling out temporarily, then producing giant swells, sometimes a riptide, sometimes only tiny waves.

"Now, picture this as a worldwide condition, Gigi. Here we have close to four billion people who want things. And everything they want is in scarce supply. There isn't enough of anything. But because everything is unequally distributed right from the start, including the people and the abilities people have, what we call the market—and that's the whole human area where people meet to exchange everything from money and cars and houses and automobiles and gasoline and food and clothes and even ideas—that whole human area acts just like the ocean. You couldn't have found a better example."

"Papa, that's so simple."

"As I told you at the beginning, Gigi, all economic ideas are really quite simple."

"I'll bet you know more than just about anybody."

"Oh, my. That isn't the least bit true. I'm really quite an ignorant man. There are many things I don't know anything about at all."

"Papa, don't say that."

"Gigi, let's clear that up. I'm ignorant. I couldn't begin to tell you of thousands of things that I know nothing whatever about. But there is a difference between being ignorant and being stupid. I'm not stupid. And neither are you. But you and I are both ignorant of many things.

"Never be ashamed of being ignorant. That is correctable by learning. While you are learning these things from me, other people are learning many other things. It will often pay you to ask them questions about the things you don't know. Nobody knows it all. Nobody. We are hemmed in by ignorance. It is the one thing all human beings share.

"But don't confuse that with being stupid. To be stupid is to insist on being ignorant. You can learn. And while you can't learn everything, you can learn a great deal. The wise man knows some things and puts them to use. The stupid man thinks he knows it all. Even as we learn, Gigi, we can keep in mind that we are merely scratching the surface. However long we live and however much we learn, there will be vast vacancies in our knowledge. Learn all you can, but be humble. It took me a long time to learn that. But I finally had to realize that I could learn something of value from nearly everyone I've ever met."

I looked at the little girl sitting so thoughtfully beside me. How trusting she was. How vulnerable. And how increasingly vulnerable I was.

An ache came to my heart. I wanted to freeze the moment, to make it endure for all time to come. But time is inexorable, and it marches on despite our wishes and our prayers.

"This is enough for now, Gigi. Think about it. And we'll talk more, later on, about the law of supply and demand."

Chapter 6

COMPETITION AND CONFLICT

"I hate him! I hate him!"

Virginia flounced into the living room, tossed her books to the ottoman, from which they cascaded to the floor, and then flung herself onto the sofa.

"That Mr. Olafson is a snark! I hate him!"

Her face was flushed. She had a respect for books, bordering on reverence. To do violence to a textbook was not like her.

"Who is Mr. Olafson and what is a snark?" I asked.

"Oh, he's one of my teachers. And if you don't know what a snark is, a snark is a twerp."

"I know better than to ask what a twerp is," I said with resignation.

"I'll tell you what a twerp is," she stormed. "He's a . . . well . . . he's a . . . . " She sputtered in frustration but no words came.

"Something most unpleasant, I'm sure," I agreed. "Let me help. A twerp is an icky, yukky snark."

"Do you know him?" Virginia asked.

"No. And it sounds as though I'd just as soon forego the pleasure. What did he do?"

"Oh, he didn't *do* anything. It's what he said."

"Do you want to tell me what he said?"

"Not really. It'll probably make you mad, too."

"Then we could be mad together."

Virginia's eyes softened. "Oh, Papa, you are such a wonderful person. And that Mr. Olafson said you were crazy. That was his exact word. Crazy. He said you are filling my head with a lot of crazy ideas."

My eyebrows went up. "Hmmm. I wonder what caused him to say that."

"Well, I was trying to explain to him about scarce resources and he said you had it all mixed up. He said there's plenty of everything if only some people weren't greedy. And he said that the law of supply and demand doesn't work. He said those are old-fashioned notions that went out of style a century ago.

"And then I tried to tell him about a foot race and how it's fair if only everyone starts off even. And he said that's where you are wrong. That the rich people start out ahead because they inherit so much money. And that we ought to take all the money away from the rich and divide it up among the poor and then everything would be fine. He said nothing is fair and that's because of greedy, selfish businessmen. He said they exploit everyone. And that you're *crazy* if you think anything else."

"What does Mr. Olafson teach?"

"Social Science. And I hate it. And I hate him, too."

"I see." I sat down on the ottoman, facing her. "Gigi, what I'm going to say is very important. Before we consider Mr. Olafson's accusation, I'd like to say something that I'm sure Mr. Olafson would agree to. It's obvious that either he or I am wrong. Since we are approaching reality from opposite directions, it is quite likely that there is an irreconcilable gap between us. But I'm sure he would agree that only the truth matters.

"So let's begin this way. Don't accept what I say because I'm your guardian or because we have a precious, valuable relationship, you and I. I could still be wrong. And don't reject what Mr. Olafson says simply because you don't like him or you don't like the way he handles his subject. Suppose he is right? What really matters is the truth."

"Papa, I *know* you're not crazy. And I *know* you tell me the truth."

"Thank you, my dear. I hope I'm not crazy. And I'm trying to tell the truth as I see it. But no one has a corner on all knowledge, hon. Remember, I told you I am ignorant in lots of areas. Of course, Mr. Olafson is, too. We all are.

"So what really matters here is your own judgment.

This is really important, Gigi. *You* have to exercise your own judgment. Too many times we tend to accept something because it apparently comes from an 'authority.' But authorities have often been wrong. There is just one thing that is never wrong. That is reality. Reality IS! So, you mustn't accept me because you view me as an authority. Nor should you accept him because you view him as an authority. Nor should you reject either of us on that ground. You must weigh the evidence yourself; use your own good judgment to find out which view of things is closer to reality."

She nodded. "But Papa, you're a lot nicer than he is." She smiled suddenly. "That's a part of reality, too."

"Thank you, Gigi. Now, let's go back and take a look. Do you remember how I defined economic goods as those things that are scarce under certain circumstances? It is those circumstances that cause us to go to work or to spend our money for things we don't have enough of. Let's think about that one point. Am I wrong in that?"

"Of course not."

"You answered too quickly, hon. Let's think about it."

"Papa, I already did think about it. Shucks." She shrugged. "Did you think I just accepted it because you said it? Well, I didn't. You *showed* it to me. About my dress. And about my pencils and the money and everything. And about the rings, too. Don't forget the rings. Both Loy's and mine. I *know* what you said is so. And that's what makes me so mad."

"Fine. Now, why do you suppose that Mr. Olafson said I was wrong?"

"Because he's a real big, fat, dummy, that's why."

"Come, dear, that's not fair. Do you suppose that Mr. Olafson has looked about him as he grew up and that he has detected some businessmen who have not exercised good judgment? You see, Gigi, a businessman is just like any other person. He, too, is acting in his own best interests as he sees them. He's human. And that means that he, too, may not always be wise.

"Here's a little exercise you might try on Mr. Olafson. Ask him if it's true that all blacks have good voices or are good athletes. Ask him if all Poles are dumb. Ask him if all the Irish are tenors. Ask him if all Chicanos are lazy.

"Let me predict what he'll say. He'll tell you that such an assumption is totally foolish. There are many blacks who can't sing a note and who aren't the least bit athletic. And he'll tell you that some Poles are very smart and that there are thousands of Irish who aren't tenors and there are hundreds of thousands of Chicanos who aren't lazy or slow in the least.

"Now, when he has said that, or something like it, ask him why he thinks that all businessmen are greedy, selfish exploiters. And if he says, well, a majority of them are, then ask him if a majority of blacks, Irish, and so on, fit into the categories you have mentioned. I think that may be an interesting intellectual challenge to Mr. Olafson and I'd like to know his reaction, if you ever do it."

Virginia squealed. "Oh, that's beautiful, Papa. I'll do it. I'll do it!" She clapped her hands. "That'll put him in his place, all right."

"Whoa, there, little lady. We're not trying to put anyone in his place. We're trying to learn the truth."

She nodded. Then her smile faded. "Papa, there is one thing he said that seemed right. About a foot race, I mean. Sure, we agreed that if everyone started out even, the race was fair no matter who won. But he said that we never do start out even. He said that was our big problem. Well, actually, he said that was *your* big problem. That you believe in competition. He said competition is wrong *because* we never start out even. So the poor never have a chance and the rich have it all their own way. And, Papa, that isn't fair!"

I nodded. "Now, that's a very good point and I'm going to agree to part of it at once. It's true, Gigi, that we don't all start out evenly. First of all, we all aren't born at the same time. So some are always older and can reasonably be expected to have learned from the larger experience they have had. Then, as I did specify in what I told you earlier, human abilities are never equally distributed.

"However, being older isn't always an advantage. When you are twelve, you are way ahead of girls who are seven or eight. Is that fair? But a girl of twenty or thirty is going to be way ahead of you."

"Papa, anyone that old isn't a *girl.*"

"Oh? What is she, then?"

"She's a woman."

"I see. Well, when you get to be my age and look back, a woman of thirty is a girl. It sort of depends on where you are when you look. So, as I look around now, I find that people who are younger than I am have an advantage over me. They have more energy. And the older I get, the larger the advantage they will have. Is that fair?"

"Sure, it is."

"You mean it's fair that an older person has less energy, but it's not fair if an older person has had more experience."

She frowned. "Papa, when you get older, I'm going to take care of you."

"I'm sure I'll need plenty of care and that's a very generous thought. But right now we're looking at competition and at being fair in a very narrow context.

"I look at competition as parallel lines of force proceeding at different rates of speed toward similar goals. In a foot race, it's important that everyone start out evenly. But that is impossible when we come to human life. It isn't really a matter of rich and poor, although those factors enter in. I haven't had time yet to talk to you about wealth and money and what those things are and how they behave.

"Actually, if you think about it, Mr. Olafson was agreeing with me when he insisted that we don't start out evenly. I stipulated that, when I pointed out the disequilibrium of distribution in all things—resources, humans, human abilities, and so on."

She leaned back and nodded vigorously. "I see that. My goodness. You agreed! Only he made it sound like you were crazy. Well, if you are, he is, too."

"I suspect neither of us is crazy. But keep this in mind. When Mr. Olafson went to school, he probably had a teacher who taught him exactly what he is teaching you. It's what he knows. So, don't be too hard on him. He's just passing along information that *seemed* right to him. Possibly he was too quick to accept some authority rather than thinking it through for himself. And that's what I want to make sure you don't do, Gigi. Always use your own best judgment. Get opposing views. That's a *good* thing. And then you weigh them and decide which comes closest to truth."

"Then life isn't very fair, is it, Papa?"

"Not in the sense of a foot race, Gigi. A foot race is a *contrived* piece of competition. You have to organize it and set it up to make it work. But *all* life is a natural kind of competition. It works all the time whether we want it to or not. It *is*. And we never start even. Some will have advantages. Some will be lucky. Some will be unlucky. Think, for instance, of babies born sickly, or lame or crippled. Through no fault of their own, they have natural handicaps. They certainly don't *deserve* a handicap in the sense that they *earned* it. They're just stuck with it. So, in life we never start even. And Mr. Olafson is right that some will begin life with more resources at their disposal than others. It's the way things are. That's reality. And you can see it, Gigi. You've already said you could.

"In real life, we don't ever start out evenly and we certainly don't finish evenly. We never will. So in the competition that is a natural kind of competition—the way life operates—the important thing is that each person, regardless of his handicaps or his talents, regardless of his wealth or his poverty, *do his best*. That's what competition is all about.

"And there's something else to keep in mind, too. I'm asking you to stand on your mental tiptoes a bit, perhaps, but I'm sure you'll see it, Gigi. Even if we don't start evenly or finish evenly, life is fair *if* we rely on voluntary actions.

"So, do the best you can with the resources you have, whatever they are. Talent, looks, money, whatever. And as you do, keep this in mind. All attainment, like all failure, is temporary. You never fail in any permanent way until you are dead. So long as you live, there will be a new day tomorrow. And you never succeed in any permanent way, either. For a new day will come and with it, challenges to whatever success you may have had.

"That's the way life can be fair, Gigi. It's fair when you let the other person be free so he can do his best. Meanwhile, if he leaves you free to do your best, then you succeed or fail as a result of your own judgment and your own energies expended.

" 'From rags to riches to rags in three generations' is an old adage. And it's the way things tend to work. And that takes me back to selfishness and the two kinds of selfishness we have. When you do your best without interfering with others, you are selfish in a good sense. And when you do your best by interfering and imposing on others, then you are being selfish in the bad sense."

"Mr. Olafson said that competition is bad because some always lose. And they don't deserve to lose."

"I can see what he's getting at, Gigi. Probably Mr. Olafson is a very sensitive person whose heart aches when he sees the distress many people face. In a sense, all of us face distress of one kind or another. And he also has undoubtedly seen instances of injustice; where one man has gained an advantage over another by force or trickery. And that's bad-selfish, as we know.

"You see, Mr. Olafson is human. He, too, wants to make profits—plus factors. But he is bordering dangerously on the idea that because there may be those who have much more than others, the cure is to impose on them by force so they are handicapped and can't perform so well. Or possibly he wants to punish those who have done bad things.

"Gigi, *you* should understand that. You reminded me—remember Loy's ring. When you took it, you were not competing fairly. You went out of a natural condition of competition and entered into conflict. And conflict and competition are opposite things. To picture conflict, I see lines of force meeting head on. That's not the same as competition. Competition consists of parallel lines of force proceeding at varying speeds toward similar goals.

"What was your goal? It was getting a ring. You obtained one ring by initiation of an act of conflict. We didn't punish you. We wanted you to think it through for yourself. And you did. So then, by quite proper competitive efforts, you went out and got another ring. You exchanged something you had that you didn't want, for money. And with the money, you got the ring. Exactly right. That's competition that hurts no one. You benefited the girl who bought your dress. She wanted the dress more than the money she gave up for it. And then you benefited the storekeeper and people in the jewelry business. The storekeeper wanted money more than he wanted the ring. And in the end, you got the benefit you wanted and you did it without hurting anyone. What's wrong with that?"

"Papa, that is just plain true."

"I think so, too, Gigi. It's the way things are. At least it is as I see it."

"You know, it's a funny thing. I'm beginning to like Mr. Olafson. Well, not really *like* him. Not like I do you. But . . . well, I guess I don't hate him any more."

"Splendid, Gigi. You see what was happening. You were beginning to get yourself into a conflict with him. Had you done so, things in his class would have gotten worse and worse. Now, perhaps, you understand him better. Compete with him in a mutual search for truth. Do your best. Show him that you can learn from him. Challenge him. But be fair. You don't have to put him in his place. You must understand him. But always do *your* best. Then you will live life fully and there will be loads and loads of plus factors for you."

"All the same, he shouldn't have called you 'crazy.' "

"You're right, Gigi. It wasn't necessary or true. But we've converted what might have been a conflict into a competitive effort. I'm going to keep on offering you ideas. I think they are right. But you must always judge them on their own merit and challenge me if you think I am wrong. Let Mr. Olafson have the same courtesy. Listen to him. You can learn from him and he can learn from you."

"Oh, Papa, he can't learn from me. He's a professor."

"Can I learn from you, Gigi?"

"I guess not."

"Wrong." I smiled wistfully. "You've taught me lots of things. And I suspect that Mr. Olafson has a class this year that will help bring out the best that is in him."

"Thank you, Papa."

"I must remember to talk to you a bit about communication of ideas, Gigi. Not now. Supper is almost ready. But many times we kind of ruin what could otherwise be a good communication. We try to tell each other what our conclusions are, rather than giving the other person the base from which we have developed our conclusions. It's possible that you did that with Mr. Olafson. Sometimes we like to beat people over the head with our conclusions. But they don't know how we got those ideas, so then they try to beat us over the head with theirs. Conflict again. Instead, if we start at the beginning and take it a step at a time, the other person can accept the premises—or at least see clearly what those premises are. And if he's reasonably intelligent, he'll reach his own conclusions and they will become as important to him as yours are to you. Curiously, when we do it that way, we often find agreement where agreement seemed impossible.

"Not that agreement is all that important. Sometimes a good healthy disagreement is very beneficial. But we'll talk about this later.

"Now, hon, I'm sure that these books on the floor are wondering what they did wrong so that you punished them."

She laughed and scrambled to her knees, putting things in order. "Books don't think, Papa. And they don't make decisions. You said so yourself."

I let my hand rest briefly on her lovely hair.

How much Virginia had taught me. Yet, not at any time had she considered herself my teacher. She taught me by being herself. By being herself, she provided the invaluable lessons I needed, not only about herself but about me.

I wondered if she benefited by my guardianship as much as I did. She had caused me to make some rather surprising discoveries about myself. Was it harder for me to learn than it was for her? Probably. When we are older, we are always conscious of what we have experienced and learned. When we are younger, the world is open and we seek to understand its mysteries.

I was certain that Virginia was absolutely frank and open with me. But was I being as open and frank with her? Was I too conscious of my age? My experience? My role as guardian, hence, my role as a superior to an inferior? Was I, in fact, playing a role, while this adorable child was simply expressing herself in all things naturally? Then who was superior and who inferior?

How does one know that he has said the right thing? Or saying the right thing, said it in the best possible way?

The truth was that I cared about her deeply. And how easily that feeling could be misconstrued. I dared not do more than play a role for I was not certain enough of my own nature to have confidence. It is only the innocent who avoid role-playing. They alone can afford the luxury of ingenuousness.

Chapter 7

PRICE AND VALUE

Virginia and I drove out Sunset Boulevard and turned into Benedict Canyon. The green lawns and the stately palms provided foreground and frame for magnificent homes, most of them white stucco, many with red tile roofs. It was her first trip to Beverly Hills.

"Everyone who lives here *has* to be a millionaire, Papa!"

"A great many wealthy people do live here, Gigi. But there are many people here who are not wealthy. We nearly always think of this city as one made up of millionaires. You'd be surprised how many have rather ordinary jobs and how many work very, very hard to be able to pay their bills."

"I'd like to live in one of these houses," Virginia said. "Do they cost much? Maybe we could afford it."

"Possibly one day we can. Right now, I'm afraid, I'd better plan on keeping us all in our rather ordinary house. At least until I get it paid for. That will take some time."

"Oh, look at that place." Gigi pointed to a palatial residence, set back from the road. "I'd like to live there."

"Douglas Fairbanks and Mary Pickford used to live around here some place. Maybe that was their home. You wouldn't remember them, Gigi. They were two of the biggest stars before pictures learned how to talk. Years ago, I used to know where many of the stars lived. But there's been so much development and so many changes, I'm not sure any more.

"I am pretty sure that place on our left is Harold Lloyd's

old place. And you wouldn't remember him, either. Up there on the hill was where John Gilbert lived. Up on the right was the home of John Barrymore and straight ahead, that rather small but quite pretty place, was the home of Rudolph Valentino."

"I have heard of Barrymore," Gigi nodded. "And Rudolph Valentino."

"They were all stars and they all made it big."

"It must be nice to be a star. Nothing to do but let people take pictures of you all day. And then to be paid so much."

"That's interesting, Gigi. Actually, the stars, the character actors, and even the bit players work very hard. When they're working. They get up early. And they study and study. And they must have an infinite amount of patience because the director will keep them going over their lines and their actions again and again and again, until their nerves are frayed and they are nearly ready to drop.

"Just like everything else, Gigi. Everyone succeeds or fails on the basis of how hard he tries, provided he has something to begin with. And there is a large measure of luck. So being in the movie industry is like anything else. You work hard. You compete. And whatever you have in the way of looks, ability, and so on, all helps.

"But if you find an actor who has an enormous amount of ability but who won't work at his profession, well, frankly, he won't succeed. Nine times out of ten, it's hard work that makes the difference in the end."

The canyon drive curved as it gained altitude. Presently we came out on Mulholland and turned left, riding the ridge in the direction of Santa Monica.

"Oh, Papa, it is lovely up here, isn't it?"

"I think so, Gigi. Let's turn off here and look across the city."

I swung the car onto a graveled overlook and stopped. A thin pall of haze marred the distant view but we could still see for miles. Above the haze, the sky was a robin's-egg blue and not a cloud was in sight.

Virginia sighed. "I hope one day I have enough money so I can buy a house up here. Wouldn't that be scrumptilious?"

"Indeed, it would be."

"I'll have to make the money myself. I don't ever want to get married."

"Fine. Nothing wrong with that. Nothing wrong with getting married, either, if you should decide to later on."

We were both silent a few minutes, gazing at the tall buildings along Wilshire and at the myriad of homes both near and far.

"Your last remark, Gigi, gives me an excellent opening if you want more of my thoughts about economics."

"Oh, goodie." She curled her legs under her and turned so she could face me. She wore a dark-blue skirt and a white blouse with a large ruffly collar. She was very pretty. "I was hoping you would, but I didn't want to ask you."

"You were saying you didn't want to get married. Splendid. No problem. And I said that getting married is no problem, either. If the right man comes along and you change your mind, that, too, could be a good thing. But what I wanted you to see is this: Whatever you do, there will always be a cost.

"We've talked about the law of supply and demand. Now this is another law. A very famous science fiction writer popularized it some time ago by using the first initials of the law to make what appears to be a meaningless word. In fact, I've found that a number of college students use it frequently. The word is TANSTAAFL." I spelled it. "Can you guess what those initials stand for?"

She shook her head.

" 'There ain't no such thing as a free lunch.' And that's very sound economic wisdom."

"You mean, food always costs money?"

"Yes. But TANSTAAFL means much more. It confirms the fact that there is nothing free. Everything has a cost. Like your decision to avoid marriage. If you decide to live your own life without a partner, there will be a number of plus factors for you. But there will also be a cost. If you ultimately decide to go the other way, again there will be plus factors, but there will also be costs. Nothing is free. You always pay.

"Going back again. We saw that all resources are scarce and unequally divided. And we also saw that goods and services don't produce themselves or move around by themselves. Everything happens because somebody decides to make them move. That's part of it. But every time anyone makes a decision to do something, that decision will cost him something. We all know that, when we go to the store. We anticipate before going that whatever we want is going to cost money. So, before we go to the store we arrange to have money or we arrange for credit, which must be redeemed later in money. Because we know that goods and services in stores will cost us something.

"But TANSTAAFL has a much grander application. It relates to every act of life. *Nothing* is free. When we decided to come on this ride this lovely morning, we both paid a price. There were other things each of us could have been doing. And in addition to the cost in your time and my time, I have to pay the cost of our gasoline and on the wear and tear to the car. You see, everything wears out. No exceptions. Nothing is permanent. Some things wear out faster than others, but everything wears out in time. Life is the only thing that renews. But even every individual life runs its course and ultimately is used up.

"So TANSTAAFL is a reminder of this fact. If you don't get married, you will gain in certain ways. Your earnings will be your own. You can do exactly as you please with your net income, without consulting anyone. You'll have only yourself to think of. And this will give you great latitude. So you won't have to put up with the personal desires of others. And you can avoid the arguments and bitterness that often arise in close relationships.

"But you may often be lonely. And if you are ill, there will be no one around to look after you. So, while there are gains, there are costs.

"The same thing works in reverse. If you get married, then you'll have to show consideration for your partner. It won't be just your wishes that matter. His will be important, too. And you'll not be able to have the same latitude in your comings and goings. But the plus factors will tie to companionship and concern. Someone else will care what happens to you. So you pay a price, but you get some plus factors, too. Nothing is free."

"I guess there is no such thing as freedom, huh, Papa."

"I wouldn't put it quite that way. There is no such thing as a cost-free decision. So nothing comes without its price. But that's not quite the way I'd define freedom. Freedom isn't the ability to avoid cost or the ability to avoid the consequences of your actions. Freedom is the ability to decide which actions you will take. And freedom is being able to act without having someone else interfere forcefully. So, freedom isn't quite the same as escaping payment. There is no escape from payment. But you can and, indeed, must and will decide just what plus factors you want. After which, you must always be prepared to pay the costs, for the costs will be there.

"Now, the reason I wanted to talk a little about this is because at the moment there is a large area of misunderstanding here. Many people have been led to believe that whatever they want, it ought to be supplied and without cost. But that is impossible. Indeed, the law of TANSTAAFL is just about as exact as a law of physics relating to energy. If you ever take physics, you'll learn that for every action in the universe, there is an equal and opposite reaction.

"Let me explain it this way. Many times parents have come to me saying, 'I've sacrificed and sacrificed to give my daughter a good education.' Sometimes I've responded to that statement with a question such as this: 'You've sacrificed! Who held the gun to your head?'

"If I ask that, they usually show a certain amount of indignation. They come back by saying, 'Of course there was no gun! But surely you know that educational costs are very high. Why, it cost me ten or maybe fifteen thousand dollars to provide for that education. And if I hadn't spent all that money on my daughter, I could have bought a fancy new car, or taken an expensive vacation in Europe, or bought a new house or new furniture, or whatever. So, I sacrificed my own wishes and my own comfort in order to give my daughter a good start in life!'

"So then I say, 'Why did you do that?'

"And they respond, 'Because that was what I *wanted* to do.'

"Then I say, 'Then you did what you wanted to do. Where's the sacrifice?' Surely we can't call an action which someone *wanted to perform*, a sacrifice."

Virginia tilted back her head and laughed. It was a delightful sound and I joined in.

"Oh, Papa! That's funny. Why are people so dumb?"

"They're not dumb, Gigi. Not at all. They actually tell me this because they want to be admired. They are really saying, 'Look what a fine person I am. I wasn't selfish! I could have done certain things for myself, but instead I did them for my daughter.' But actually, if you analyze it, they were acting in their own best interests at the time. They weighed the cost of having an educated daughter against the costs of the car, the vacation, or whatever else they wanted, and then they decided that the plus factors of an educated daughter were *larger* than the plus factors of getting the new car. So they did act selfishly, and in their own best interest, as they saw it at the time. But of course they couldn't escape the costs.

"You see, Gigi, resources are very scarce. Each of us has a limited amount of time, a limited amount of energy, a limited amount of skills, a limited amount of money and goods. And that's all we have. Each of us has many places to put our resources. But we have a very limited supply of resources. So we have to select with great care those actions which, to us, have the largest number of plus factors, and the lowest cost — *as we see it*."

Virginia sat very still. "There are some exceptions to that, aren't there, Papa?"

"I don't think so, hon. Can you give me one?"

"Well, I get lots of things from you for free. They don't cost me anything."

"I see what you mean. Actually, Gigi, it is always possible for someone else to pay a cost. But it is not possible for the cost to remain unpaid. There is no such thing, even for an instant, as an unpaid bill. For instance, I use credit to a certain extent. I charge things at the store. It might appear, at that moment, that I had gotten something for nothing. Actually, by using credit I am asking the storekeeper to pay my bill for me right then because I promise to pay him later on. Now, what would happen if I didn't pay the bill? The goods would still be paid for. It's just that I didn't pay. The storekeeper had to pay.

"We use credit as a kind of comfort cushion. And we

only keep our credit because in the end we make the payment. If a person didn't pay his bills, storekeepers would be stuck and have to make the payments. And if the storekeepers didn't pay, the wholesalers would be stuck. And so on back to natural resources and the payment to the people who own them and produce them."

"But some things are free, aren't they, Papa? I mean, people can give you things and you don't have to pay."

"Of course, Gigi. Actually, we all enjoy doing that to some degree with and for the people we like. That's why we give parties. The host pays the bill and the guests come at the expense of the host. But the bill is paid by someone somewhere along the line. So while it is possible for you to stick someone else with a cost, it is not possible for that cost to go unpaid."

"Am I sticking you with my costs, Papa?"

"Oh, dear. That was an unfortunate choice of words, wasn't it. No, indeed. You are an invited guest. I'm *not* stuck in the least. Actually, I view you as an investment. I'm putting a certain amount of time, energy, ideas, and money into you so that later on, you'll be able to make your own way successfully in the world."

"Why, Papa? I'm not your daughter."

"If you were my daughter, I would still treat you the same way. Or at least I should. A daughter would be an invited guest, just as you are. But, of course, to some degree there is a cost to you, or to a daughter. While you live in my house, you must agree to my rules as to how the household will run. You may not like some of them. But as long as you are my guest, you must treat me with certain consideration in exchange for the bills I'm paying for you. That's how it works. So, even to you, the free things I give you aren't entirely free. See what I mean?"

"I sure see that. Like the rule that I go to bed at ten o'clock. Papa, that's much too early."

"When you are paying the bills, Gigi, you can stay up as long as you like. When I pay them, and in my house where you are my guest, you pay by being considerate of my wishes."

"Then it really is fair, isn't it?"

"Of course it is. Loy and I wanted you to come. You

did. And I think it was a very wise move on our parts. Possibly the best investment I ever made."

"Really, Papa?"

"Really."

"That makes me feel very good. I didn't think of myself as a guest."

"I'm surprised to hear that."

"Well, I guess I did, too. It's just that I understand it better. Guests are supposed to have good manners and be polite and considerate, aren't they?"

"Of course."

"Well, I can see that that's fair."

"Splendid. Now, the problem we find today, Gigi, is that some people feel imposed upon by reality. And they go into a state of rebellion. They don't see why they don't have enough money to pay for their daughter's education, plus the car, plus the vacation, plus whatever else they want. They make invidious comparisons, with people who they imagine have a great deal more money than they have."

"Papa, what's invidious?"

"Oops! Another big word. It means odious, unpleasant. What I mean is that a great many people become envious. And they spend a lot of their time being angry at other people who seem to have more, and then they strike out against society because they think that other people have everything they want and that society is imposing on them because they don't have everything they want."

"Well, some people do have more."

"True enough. We've been through that, Gigi. And that brings us back to good-selfish and bad-selfish. People who want more and go to work to get more, or save up their money so they can afford the things they want, are being productive, constructive, and good-selfish. But when people become bad-selfish, then they become envious of others. Instead of mending their own fortunes, they spend their time trying to take things away from others. And they feel that life isn't being fair with them.

"But however much they have, they will always have to go without. I know that seems unbelievable. But it's true. I have known a number of people who, by my standards, were rich. They had a great deal more than I do. But, they, too, were going without lots of things. Nobody gets it all. Nobody gets everything he wants.

"You see, even the costs of making money are very high. The man who decides to become very wealthy pays a price for that decision. He concentrates so totally on his business that he often neglects wife, children, personal pleasures, and just about everything else. People often say that rich people are unhappy people. But that isn't quite true. What they recognize is that rich people have a different scale of values than others. And because they assume that everybody's value will be the same as theirs, they imagine that a person who devotes himself to nothing but making money is unhappy. He is paying a price that *they* wouldn't want to pay. But he may be happy in his own way. No one else is compelling him to live that way. He is doing that which he wants to do but he is paying the price. That's the way things are."

"You know, Papa, everything you say makes so much sense. Actually, it's kind of obvious, isn't it? Like the way I didn't value my skirt. I was surprised when I found so many other girls thought it was a pretty skirt."

"Value is easy to understand once you grasp that none of us will value things equally. But people are often in rebellion against the obvious because they really don't like the way reality is. However, rebellion against reality is a sad kind of rebellion. To rebel against injustice, against evil, these are good rebellions. But to rebel against reality is futile and silly. It would be like bursting into tears because the sun comes up. Or because things fall to the floor if we let go of them."

"I like economics. I really do. It isn't about arithmetic at all."

"The basic rules aren't, Gigi. But there is one other point I want to make here. It'll only take a minute. When you have a resource and decide what to do with it, whether it's time, money, energy, or whatever, you make a total commitment. What I'm saying is that you can't have your cake and eat it, too. If you eat it, it's gone. If you save it, then you didn't eat it. It's that simple.

"But while it's simple and obvious, it is also profound.

Many people think you can spend a dollar two or three times. You can't. When you spend the dollar, that dollar is gone. It's like time. The hour or more we are spending on this little drive is an hour that will never come back again. We live life a moment at a time and we don't duplicate. You can't go back.

"So it behooves each of us to learn as much as we can and to exercise all the good judgment we can so that we dispose of our scarce resources in the most advantageous way possible. The wiser we are and the more careful we are, the more plus factors we'll have and the lower the costs will be."

"Papa." A small hand groped my way and I took it. "Do you think I'll ever be able to afford a fine house up here? I really love it."

"I can only say, hon, that it's up to you. There will be plenty of costs involved. Nothing is free. TANSTAAFL. But if it means enough to you, then you'll work hard enough and save up enough money so you can. It certainly isn't impossible at all."

"Then let's go home. I want to tell Loy where I'm going to live."

I turned the car to the west and we drove home, taking Mulholland as far as possible. It was a beautiful ride.

Chapter 8

HOW TO

"Do you know how to play chess?" Virginia asked.

I looked up from a stack of papers. "Well, I used to play quite a good deal. It's been years. I remember the moves, of course. But I'm terribly rusty."

"I'm learning how to play. It's a wonderful game."

"Do they teach chess in school now?"

"Oh, no, Papa. But there's someone in school who is teaching me."

"I see." My eyes were on her face but I was thinking of the game.

Slowly, a crimson tide engulfed her neck and features.

"Who is teaching you?"

"Someone at school."

"Does the someone have a name?"

She nodded and the flush deepened.

"Do I know her?"

She shook her head. Dropping her voice she said, "It's not a her, it's a him."

"What?"

"It's a boy."

"I see. Does the boy have a name?"

Again she nodded. "It's Henry."

"Just Henry? Nothing more?"

"Henry O'Neill."

Speaking that name was a confessional.

"When do you play?"

"In study period."

"Do you have time in study period for playing chess?"

"Oh, sure. Henry sits across from me. And he has this darling little chess set with teentsie-weentsie pieces and he puts it on the side of his desk. And then he makes a move and when I'm ready, I reach across the aisle and make my move. And it's lots of fun."

"I'm sure it is. But it does take lots of concentration. I should think it might interfere with your studies."

"Oh, it doesn't at all, Papa. Of course, I'm not very good. Henry always beats me."

"Is he good at it?"

"Oh, yes. He's real smart."

"I'm glad you're learning chess, Gigi. I'm told it's the one game in which the element of luck is totally absent. But I'm surprised you like it. It's mathematically precise. And you don't like math."

"Henry likes it and I do, too."

I nodded. I looked at my watch. Then I looked down trying to find my place in the manuscript.

"Papa, would you play me a game? I mean, do you have a set and will you play me?"

"Yes, I have a set. It was given to me by a student of mine from the Philippines. And it's a very beautiful one. But I do have to finish this work."

"Tell me where the set is and I can set it up while you finish."

"Gigi, this work is quite extensive. It may take quite a while."

"I'll be patient, Papa. I'll just wait."

Suddenly, I didn't think very favorably of Henry O'Neill. I pushed the papers aside.

"The set is in the cabinet over there. It's a fold-out board and the pieces are inside. You can set it up here on the desk. I can see that there'll be no more work for me until we play."

She chortled, and danced over to the cabinet. In a moment, the set was located and the pieces put into place. I kept a pawn of each color.

"Which hand do you want, Gigi?"

"Oh, that's what Henry does, too. He always lets me choose."

Her fingers brushed the back of my right hand. How

soft and gentle they were.

"I'll take that hand."

The whites were hers.

"You have the first move."

"I know."

She used the conventional opening and I followed with my king's pawn. Several fairly rapid moves followed as we developed our game plans.

"Gigi, I want you to know that I won't pull any punches. I'll beat you if I can. Even though you may be a beginner, I shall play you for all I'm able."

She was concentrating and didn't respond. The study was silent as we got deeper into the game. Finally, I pinned one of her rooks and gained a distinct advantage. She moved hastily and I straightened up.

"Are you sure you want to make that move, Gigi? I'll let you take it back."

"You said you'd beat me if you could, Papa. I like my move."

My queen swept across the board and captured her rook.

She shrilled in joy, her hand hovering a moment over the ranked combatants. Then one of her knights, which I had failed to take into consideration, leaped over a pawn.

"Checkmate! Checkmate! Oh, I beat you, I beat you!"

The little minx had, at that. I studied the board ruefully.

"My gosh, Gigi. That's a good move. I didn't see it coming."

"You didn't think I could, did you? But I did! I beat you!"

"Where did you learn that move?"

"Henry showed it to me. He told me that if I developed my game correctly and got your attention diverted, you'd go whooping after my castle and I'd be able to checkmate. And you did and I did."

My laugh may have sounded hollow. "Henry O'Neill seems to have it figured out right down to the wire."

"He has, Papa. He sure has. Oh, he's terribly, terribly brilliant."

"I believe it."

"Didn't I play well?"

"Far better than I did, I'm afraid. I'll have to practice up. Next time, I won't be so easy." I started to put the pieces away.

"Oh, please, Papa, leave them. Leave them that way!"

"Not on your life, young lady. I don't want to memorialize my defeat. I can just see you marching in here day after day to point to the board and lord it over me."

"That's not it at all, Papa. I want to be able to show Henry."

"How do you propose doing that? You aren't thinking of carrying the board this way to school, are you?"

" 'Course not, silly. I thought that maybe I could invite Henry out, sometime. And then he could see how I did it with his own eyes."

"I have a better idea. Why not make a copy of the board with the pieces in this particular situation? Then you could take it to school if you wished."

"Don't you want Henry to come out?"

"As a matter of fact, it might be a good idea if Henry came out so I could meet him. He sounds like someone I had better get to know."

"Oh, you'll like him, Papa. You really will."

"You're very fond of him, aren't you, Gigi?"

She nodded and her eyes were bright.

"All right. Then perhaps you had best invite him sometime. If you like him that much, he must have many fine qualities." I could think of several he didn't have.

"Then let me take the board to my room. I'll make a chart and put the pieces on it like you said."

"Fine. Then I'll get back to work."

She marched away with the scene of my defeat carefully in place, and I turned to my papers.

In a few minutes she was back again. She halted a few steps from my desk, put her hands behind her back like a soldier at parade-rest, and waited.

I could feel her eyes on me and I sighed and looked up again.

"Yes, Gigi?"

"Will you talk to me some more?"

"What about?"

"I thought maybe you'd like to give me another lesson in economics."

"I thought that chess had captured your attention."

"Of course not, Papa. I have to learn as much as I can. You see, I'm explaining economics to Henry. And he doesn't understand it at all. It's like you said. He's ignorant in that area, just as you are in chess."

"I see." I hadn't realized the extent of my ignorance before. "Very well, Gigi. As a matter of fact, my ideas are so routed that I'd be well advised to quit what I'm doing, for the time being. I think it's time for me to explain how we put the pieces together."

"Is it like chess?"

"Not at all."

"Well, you said, 'put the pieces together.' "

"Hon, get a chair. And while you're at it, better bring back the chess set and put it away. That is, if you have your chart finished."

"Oh, certainly. I forgot. I can borrow it again when Henry comes."

She dashed away and presently reappeared with the folded board, which she returned to the cabinet. Then she sat next to me.

I said nothing. A young man named Henry O'Neill whom I didn't even know was sitting between us. And I resented it. I realized just how precious she had become. I had the evidence that time was passing and days with Virginia were surely numbered.

"Aren't you going to say anything, Papa?"

"Of course. Just marshaling my thoughts. I have to think how to begin. Let's look at it this way. The world we live on is a great big ball of natural resources."

"And all of them are scarce and unequally divided," she said. "I already know that."

"Right. But there's something else. Very few of the resources are in a form which is useful to us. For example, we use food. But in order to have food we can eat, we have to clean it and season and prepare it. And we like to make combinations of different kinds of food. So a great deal of work is necessary or we don't eat well at all.

"Another item in common demand is wood. Wood

comes from trees. In order to get at the wood, we have to cut down the trees and saw them into boards and then use the boards to put things together the way we want them. And we dig into the earth looking for metals. And we drill to find oil.

"What I am saying is that in order to make use of the natural resources, a great deal of work must be done."

"I see that, Papa. It's like TANSTAAFL."

"Right. We have to work for everything.

"Now, there are only three things available to us by means of which we can convert what we find, or raise, into something useful. Early scholars called them *land*, *labor*, and *capital*. But that can be a little confusing. Instead of saying land, I'm going to say *natural resources*. That broadens it a bit. We use the land, sure. But we use the things that come from the land. And we use air and water and fire. Natural resources covers it all. All the metals, the minerals, the growing things, the animals, all these things are natural resources. Nature has provided them. We can assist nature by planting more growing things. And we can assist nature by raising cattle, sheep, hogs, and chickens. Indeed, we must keep doing this, for without human effort here, we would quickly run out of food supplies.

"But there's an interesting fact to keep in mind. In a final sense, we never really use anything up. We convert the things we raise from a form they come in, to some other form. Nothing is ever really lost."

"Oh, no, Papa. You can't mean that. What about oil? We're using that up and when it's gone, there won't be any more."

"You're right, Gigi. We convert the raw petroleum into dozens of other, more useful commodities—more useful to us than the fossilized residue that comes to us when we drill. And, of course, there are limited amounts of fossil fuels. When they are all gone, they will be gone for good.

"But that doesn't mean that we'll have to run out of energy. The entire universe is nothing but energy in varying forms. We have to learn to convert energy from various sources into humanly useful energy, one way or another.

"For example, more than a hundred years ago, the

people in Europe and America relied on whale oil for lighting and even for heating. There were hundreds of thousands of whales. Today, there are only a few. They've been hunted down and converted into energy. Today, the whales are making a small comeback. But it will take many years before they are plentiful again, if they ever are. The same thing will happen to fossil fuels such as oil and coal. We haven't learned yet how to convert energy from common sand or from garbage and trash, things which we have in plentiful supply. But we're working on it. And one day we may learn how to do a really good job of getting energy from sunlight and from atoms. Of course, even the sun will cool off in time. Nothing is forever. Change is a constant. Everything changes. But we must obtain energy or perish. It takes energy to keep us alive. You and I are like furnaces. To keep us running, we have to stoke up on food, which is our fuel."

"I remember that part, Papa. From biology."

"Good. So we understand resources. Natural resources.

"Next, we have *labor*. That word, unfortunately, brings to mind a man, naked to the waist, doing hard manual toil of some sort. So I'm going to call this particular item *human energy* instead of labor. You see, man is the actor; the decision-maker, the doer. And when I speak of human energy, I will mean *anything at all in the form of work* that a person performs. Thinking toward the attainment of a goal is work—labor. Using one's head, one's skills, or one's back muscles—each can be a form of labor. And the time we spend, the amount of knowledge we bring to bear, and so on, all relate to human energy. All these things make up the human-energy package and provide the second item in the trilogy of production.

"Finally, there's *capital*. And that's a very confusing word, so instead of using it, I'm going to say *tools*. That's what capital really is: tools.

"Isn't money capital?"

"No, it isn't. We'll talk about money some other time. Let me simply say that money is a medium of exchange; a transfer agent. The person who has money could decide to spend it for food. Or he could decide to make an investment; he could buy a tool of some kind. As long as he has money, he has broad choices open to him. Money spent on a tool is called a capital investment. So, let's keep it simple and call our third package tools.

"So we have three packages to work with: natural resources, human energy, and tools. Those are the only packages we have. By putting those pieces together, we produce everything we have in the way of a material good or service of some kind. It doesn't make any difference whether we are building houses, raising carrots, manufacturing bobby-pins, or providing hair cuts. Those are the three things at our disposal: natural resources, human energy, and tools.

"Man wants something. Remember, we are all wanting creatures. We all want plus factors. So we begin by looking to nature to supply us with what we want. We live off the resources of this planet.

"Let's suppose a man who wants to build a home for himself. One of the cheapest and simplest kinds would be a log house. So, this man is in a place where there are trees and he wants to build a house. What does he do first?"

"Well, he cuts down some trees."

"Correct. But how can he do that?"

"He just cuts them down, that's all."

"What with, Gigi? Does he chop the tree down with his bare hands? Or does he gnaw the tree down with his teeth, or claw it down with his finger nails?"

"He uses an axe, of course."

"Ah. An axe. Now, where does he get the axe?"

"He goes to the store and buys one."

"Think back—before there were stores. How would you go about getting an axe if there were no stores?"

"Oh. Well, I guess I'd have to make one."

"Tell me about that, Gigi. How would you go about making an axe?"

"Well, I'd have to dig up the iron ore, first."

"Where would you go to do that, hon?"

"Golly, I don't know. Yes, I do, too. There's iron ore in Minnesota. I remember from geography. It's in the Messahabbi Range."

"I think you mean the Messabi. Fine. And there are a few other places on earth where you might find it. But think of what is involved. If you wanted to make just a simple thing like an axe, you'd have to look for the ore, mine it, smelt it, convert the iron into steel, forge it, put a cutting edge on it. Then you'd have to get a handle of some kind. It might take you years to do this if you had to do it all by yourself. Fortunately, you and I can go to the store and find an assortment of axes to choose from. But there's no magic about it. Thousands of people worked for many years, doing all those things, so today we don't have to make our own axes. The cost of the first axe would have been tremendous. Today, we take advantage of all those earlier costs that have been met by others. We just go to a store and, with a few dollars, buy an axe.

"But bear in mind that without an axe, the man wanting to build a house would be helpless. He's not strong enough to pull the trees up by the roots. Without a tool, the trees would just continue to stand there and the man would have to live without shelter.

"This is not only true for axes and the other things necessary to build houses. It's true all the way around. Man—human energy personified—goes to work on the natural resources, with the tools.

"To begin with, all the tools were crude and badly made. The first axe was made of stone and it wouldn't cut very well. There wasn't even a handle. But gradually, men continued working and improved the axe, and finally we have, not only the axe, but the saw, and now power saws.

"Let's look around here in the study. Think of all the tools we have right here that make things easier for us. Take the lights, for instance. To begin with, man went to bed when it got dark. Or he built a fire. Gradually, he came up with improvements—candles, lamps, and finally the electric light. All those are tools.

"Look at my desk. It's a tool. Without it, I'd have to have everything on the floor or in my lap.

"And the chairs we are on. Without them, we'd be squatting, or sitting on the floor.

"And look at my typewriter. What a fantastic tool that is. But even my fountain pen is a tool. And before we had them, we used to pull quills from a goose or a pheasant and form a nib with what we call a 'pen-knife.' That is, if we had the knife.

"The books over there are tools—tools of information and knowledge gathered by others. And the bookcase that holds them—that's a tool.

"This house is a tool and everything in it is a tool. Our beds, our mirrors, the coat hangers in the closet, all are tools. And we have a furnace which is a tool. And some people have air conditioning, another tool.

"We have a cooking range and an oven and pots and pans and can openers and dishes and knives and forks and spoons. Everything we have makes it possible for us to live, and live in some degree of comfort and security. Now, suppose we had to make all those things ourselves! How much do you think we'd have?"

"Golly! Is everything a tool?"

"We have only three packages of things, Gigi. Natural resources, human energy, and tools. Aside from fresh groceries and possibly a few items of decor which are in their natural state as yet, and thus in the first category, everything else in the house is either human or it's a tool. That's all there is."

"Wow! Man, oh, man. I never thought of it that way."

"So that's how we get everything we want in the way of a good or service. Man begins by making a tool. Then he applies the tool to natural resources to help him make other tools. So, there's a whole industry specializing in making tool-making tools. And then there are consumer-type tools, which is what we've been talking about.

"Bear in mind that nothing in the way of a tool came into its present form without the expenditure of human energy, the use of resources, and the assistance of tools."

I had her full attention and her eyes were big as she considered the scope of my remarks.

"Some people at school say we have too many tools. They say we are using up everything and there won't be anything left for future generations."

"I know. I read it in newspapers and see it on television. But remember the other day we talked about what would happen if a law were passed banning the automobile? We saw what would happen."

"I remember. And it's true in other areas, too, isn't

it, Papa?"

"Of course it is. You see, one of the greatest lessons we have learned on this planet is a derivative of understanding the three packages we work with. It's called a *division of labor*.

"Back in the early days, if a man wanted a plow, he had to make it himself. And if he wanted a house, he had to build it. If he wanted something to eat, he had to plant a field, first clearing it and then plowing, and caring for it until the crop was ripe. Or he had to raise food animals and ride herd on them until they were ready for slaughter. Our pioneer ancestors were busy from morning to night and they got up early and stayed up late, just to make the basic things they had to have in order to stay alive.

"But once we began to understand that tools could be used to make other tools—and most especially when we discovered how to use the wind, and the power of falling water, and the energy from heat—then we replaced a lot of human muscular energy with human intellectual energy in the providing and harnessing of these other forms of energy. And by doing that, for the first time in human experience men began to live reasonably well and with some expectancy that life could be pleasant and something other than hard, back-breaking toil, day after day.

"When we discovered how to work effectively, we stopped being 'jacks-of-all-trades.' We began to specialize. If a group of men did nothing but build houses, they soon learned how to make better houses than the man who only built one in his life. And they found that by specializing and doing just one thing, and by using tools and forms of energy other than human, we could create and produce vast new tools which we began to use in innumerable ways.

"Thus, we learned that the better the tool and the more effective the energy applied with the tool, the more goods and services we could have. We discovered that tools multiplied the effectiveness of human energy. Many tools do the work of ten or fifty or a hundred men."

"I know that, Papa. Henry says that, too. And he says that's what's wrong. We've got so many tools that do so many things that the tools are taking over and throwing people out of work."

I looked at her carefully. "I don't like to contradict your friend. Especially since he's not here to defend his position. But the fact is, Gigi, that there are no jobs at all without tools. Every job in the world is tool-connected. There aren't any exceptions. Of course, it's true that when a new tool is introduced, right at the place where that tool is applied to the job, some people may be 'dis-employed.' I use that term rather than *unemployed* because, in fact, *more* employment occurs just on account of that tool. While the tool displaces some, it causes jobs for others who make that tool—and for those who sell it and who service it. And since tools do a better job than we do by hand with our very limited time and energy, we begin to reduce the critical scarcity of all those scarce things we've been talking about.

"Actually, Gigi, we still don't have enough tools. It is through tools that scarcities are substantially reduced. Of course, we can't eliminate scarcity altogether. But with the aid of tools we do the best job. Why, hon, no one could sweep a floor, or dust a chair, or sell an insurance policy, or trim a beard, or raise a carrot, or publish a book, without tools.

"Like the man who wanted the log house—he found he was helpless until he got tools into his hands which he could use. The better the tools, and the more efficient the energy applied, the more that can be produced and the quicker it can be done."

"Then tools are our friends, aren't they?"

"Certainly. One of the most important friends we have. A school is a tool. And think of all the tools in the school."

"Papa, that's very interesting. I am going to have to explain that to Henry."

"Splendid. He can improve your chess game and you can improve his understanding of economics."

She clapped her hands. "Oh, good." She jumped up and pushed the chair back to its place on the far side of the desk. "I can hardly wait to talk to him. Boy, will I have some things to explain to him."

I nodded.

"The three packages are natural resources, human energy, and tools." She was a picture of triumph.

"Right."

"I'll remember." She danced out of my sight down the hallway.

I began to wonder about the relative value of chess compared to a knowledge of economics.

But I didn't need to wonder. Neither chess nor economics had anything to do with it. It was the relative value of youth versus age. Time is immutable. And in time, life richly endows the young. Time wins all contests. The time of the teacher is short. The time for independence and non-interference is long.

Chapter 9

SELF-HELP HELPS OTHERS

For the next three weeks, nothing further was said about economics. Virginia was increasingly active at school and became involved in a number of extra-curricular activities.

Henry O'Neill made his masculine debut at our dinner table one evening. He was all knees and elbows, a string bean, uncomfortable in suit and shirt with tie. His hair was dark red, trained to lie to the left and face rear, except for one patch in revolt which persisted in pointing forward and to the right. His freckles were so close together that at times I suspected he had suddenly sprouted a full red beard. His fingers were long and slender and his wrists protruded from their sleeves like tie rods in a piston engine. He was mathematically precocious but otherwise about what I had anticipated.

After dinner, I dodged the challenge to a chess match and retreated to a corner. Virginia hung on his every word during that evening.

In the days that followed, she was a happy girl. Her face glowed with joy each morning. Her return from school each day was a victorious entry, like a Caesar entering Rome. She chattered endlessly with Loy about whatever it is women talk about. I brought up the subject of economics once or twice, whereupon I was scolded by Loy for seeking to intrude and shrugged off by Virginia, who clearly had her mind elsewhere.

Then, one evening, Virginia came home just at dinner time. She had apparently hoped to avoid attention by using the rear entrance. Finding us already seated, she hesitated, then continued through the dining room.

Her face was such a battleground of emotion that I was startled. The redness of her eyes and the tear streaks on her cheeks showed where the cavalry of tragedy had swept down seeking to break her heart.

I started to speak, but a look from Loy and I snapped my jaw shut. We heard her door close softly. The two of us ate alone. Sometime later, I went to her room.

After getting no response to several knocks, I tried the knob. The door opened and I went in. Virginia was sprawled across the bed, her face buried in a pillow.

I spoke very quietly. "Gigi, it's Papa. Is there anything I can do?"

She stiffened and then shook her head violently. A subdued moan came through the cushion and my heart was tugged forward and tried to escape between my ribs.

"Oh, hon. I'm so sorry. I don't mean to intrude. But talking is usually helpful. Do you want to tell me about it? Or would you rather have Loy to talk to? Maybe if you could talk about it, you'd make it go away."

There was a moment of silence. Then she raised herself to a sitting position and faced me. Her hair was disheveled and her eyes glared accusingly.

"Henry and me have busted up. And he'll never have anything to do with me again. And it's all your fault!" She spat out the last words and her eyes had a look of hurt that stabbed at my earlier jealousy.

"My fault! What did I do?"

"Well, you didn't like him, Papa. Don't deny it. He's very sensitive and he could tell. And we got to arguing over economics and he said that economics is an emperor study and not at all what you said it was. And he said you and your kind are the big problem. He said you're part of the petty boreswazee, and that all you do is take the side of the privileged classes. You just stand up for the rich people and don't care a hoot about the poor.

"And he said that the capitalist classes are the exploiters and are taking advantage of everyone else. And I stood up for you and said you weren't like that at all. And he said that maybe *you* weren't, yourself, but it's your kind that cause all the problems. And he's going to get to be president and when he does, he's going to pass laws to put all your kind in prison and take away everything you have and give it to the poor.

"And then we broke up. And I slapped his face and now he'll never speak to me again!"

"I am terribly sorry, Gigi. But it's not true that I didn't like him."

"Papa, don't say that! You didn't! Don't lie. Oh, please don't lie! You didn't like him."

"I'm not lying, Gigi. It's true I wasn't particularly attracted to him, but that is a long way from disliking him. And perhaps I misjudged him. I thought he was rather conceited. Maybe I just didn't like the competition. But, Gigi, if he had wanted to, he could have called again and we might have gotten to know each other better."

"He *did* call on you, Papa. It was *your* turn to call on him. And you didn't!"

"Well, now, that is certainly true."

"Why, Papa? Why?"

"I guess I didn't see any need to do that. As a matter of fact, Gigi, you'll probably have a great many boy friends before you ultimately find one that you wish to marry. Besides, you told me you weren't planning on getting married. So why should I go to any great trouble to visit a young man who obviously wasn't going to have any permanent or lasting relationship with you?"

She burst into tears. "I changed my mind. Henry and I were going to be married. And now we never will! Oh, I . . . I'm just so miserable!"

"I see. But you didn't tell me that, did you? How was I to know?"

She stared at me in consternation. "Oh, that's so! That *is* so. I didn't tell you. Oh, Papa, then it's all *my* fault!" A new burst of tears brought her hands to her face.

"Gigi, what happened is nobody's 'fault' at all. I'm sure Henry is a fine young man."

"How can you say that when he's been so beastly to me?"

"Sweetheart, you're getting me totally confused. I think you are free of blame, although I don't know that I'd recommend slapping someone's face when you have an argument. And I rather suspect that the subject of economics, which is what you and he apparently argued about, wasn't the *real* reason for your disagreement. If Henry had loved you, he would have tried harder to understand your position. And if you had loved him, you would have tried harder to understand his. And you might even have enlisted my help so that you could sustain your position better."

"But I did so, love him!"

"Hon, I am in no position to speak with authority about your emotions. They are yours and only you know how you felt."

"I slapped his face because he deserved it! He said terrible things about you, Papa. Oh, I hate him!" She shuddered in revulsion.

"Come, hon. Dry your eyes. If you hate him, then you can forget him. If you love him, then I'm sure things can be straightened out, especially if he really cares for you."

Ultimate tragedy etched her face anew. She spoke very quietly. "Oh, no, Papa. It's all over. Henry is being transferred. His family is moving away. His father got a job in another state and they're moving. They don't understand him, either. He wanted to stay and set up an apartment on his own. But his parents don't understand. They are making him go with them. They don't seem to realize that he's grown up and can manage quite nicely without them."

"Gigi, you say his parents don't understand him, *either*. Does that mean that we don't understand you?"

She looked at me puzzled. "That's strange, Papa. I don't think that's true. Henry said that. He said you didn't understand me at all."

"Before he showed up, I thought we, you and I, had a very special, wonderful relationship."

"Oh, we did. We did!"

"Good. I always thought so. Tell you what. Why don't you splash some cold water on your face and freshen up a bit? You'll feel better. Then, have something to eat if you wish. When you're quite ready, come to the living room. I've got some things to read, but I'd like to tell you a story."

"You mean, you want to tell me more about economics,

don't you?"

"Well, yes. But I want to do it by telling you a little story. It'll be a make-believe story. Like the ones I used to tell you. Remember?"

"Papa, am I still your little girl?"

"Gigi, I'm not certain that you are a little girl any longer. Tragedy makes us all mature and you are facing one. But you are certainly my girl until you decide otherwise. Is that okay?"

"I want to be your *little* girl." A smile peeked through the overcast.

"Then that is what you are." I bent over and kissed her tear stains. "See you in a bit."

Later, with both of us on the sofa, I put my arm around her and began. Her eyes were still red, but she was apparently calm.

"I must start by saying that I'm indebted to an article I read in a magazine for this story. But I'm going to tell it to you in my own words. However, I wanted you to know that this story isn't original with me.

"Once upon a time, a tribe of people lived together in small huts at the base of a very tall hill. There were exactly one hundred people in this tribe and they were all adults."

"How sad," Virginia said. "Was something wrong with them?"

"Actually," I said, "Henry has caused me to eliminate the children. I've always left the children in it before. But I'd better remove them for now. Henry said that economics is an empirical study. You said 'emperor,' but I knew what you meant: a way of looking at things based on experience rather than on theory or scientific analysis. And incidentally, the term you used, *bourgeoisie* — that comes from the French and means the people who live in the town. By implication it also means that they own property. The people in my story could be thought of as proletariat. Although they lived in a community, they comprised a group of hunters and foragers and did not own property.

"Why did they live at the bottom of the hill, Papa?" She snuggled warmly against me and I gave her an affectionate squeeze.

"The hill was right near the ocean and they lived

behind it to protect themselves from the strong winds that came in from the open water. And they lived there because they survived on a food economy based on what they could catch in the sea. They ate fish and crabs and sea gulls. And so they lived at the bottom of the hill, for otherwise they would have had to walk up and down the hill to go to and from their huts.

"Nearby was a small forest. And they hunted in there, too, and sometimes caught a deer and in season they could garner nuts and berries. So they had a pretty good life, all things considered. But they did have a problem.

"You see, the only fresh water came from a spring that bubbled to the surface at the very top of this high hill. From there, the water plunged in a series of waterfalls down into the ocean. So to give my story an empirical approach, I will now specify that each of the villagers consumed one pailful of water every day. So, once a day, each villager had to climb to the top of the hill to fill his pail with water. It took him an hour and a half to make the climb, but only thirty minutes to come down again. This meant that each villager spent two hours a day getting his own water supply. So, as even you and I can figure, the entire village of a hundred people used up two hundred hours every day getting their supplies of drinking water."

Virginia chuckled. "I can figure easy sums like that."

"Fine. We can bring the children back again when I've finished my story. I'm only removing them for the time being to keep everything nice and even. You see, if we bring in children, some of the people might have to make two trips to get water and that would complicate the figures. So I'm arbitrarily sending the children away for the evening and insisting that each one of the villagers got exactly one pail of water each day."

"I see."

"One of the villagers was a very intelligent man."

"Was he an economist?"

"Not really. Probably he was a philosopher. Anyone can be a philosopher. One day after he had climbed the hill and sat down on a rock to catch his breath, he got to thinking about the water, and he noticed a very interesting thing. Water always runs down hill."

"Oh, Papa, I know who he is. That's Sir Isaac Newton. But you have to have him under an apple tree."

"Not this particular Newton. He figured out the law of gravity by watching the behavior of water. But there weren't any newspapers in the area so he didn't get to be famous. In thinking about the water, he realized that the flow from the stream ran down the hill on the ocean side, away from the village. What if he could do something to make the water run the other way? What if he could convince the gods who lived in the water and made it run down hill, to change the channel for the water and get it to run down the hill on the village side? If the water came down into the village, every person in the village could be saved two hours of work every day."

"Nobody else had figured that out?"

"Nobody. Just this one man figured it out."

"Papa, there aren't any gods in the water, are there?"

"We don't think so. But this early Mr. Newton thought so. After dabbling about in the water for a bit, he figured out that if he dammed up the stream where it plunged down the hill, and dug a channel on the other side, the water would go that way. And the gods in the stream wouldn't really mind. They'd still let the water run down hill."

"Papa, that's really very simple."

"Sure, it is. Nearly all really good ideas are quite simple, although sometimes we find out about them in very complicated and strange ways.

"Now, the hero of our story had a problem. How was he going to build the dam and dig the channel? He realized he couldn't do it with his bare hands. He'd have to have a tool. But there weren't any. The people in the village had invented huts and fishhooks and spears and baskets. And they all had pails. But what he needed was a pick and shovel. And of course they didn't exist.

"So he sat down and thought through the problem. It took him exactly fifty hours to design the first pick and the first shovel. And all he had done was to *think*. But while he was concentrating on that, he didn't have time to do other things. So he reduced the amount of time he spent hunting and foraging and fishing, and spent a part of his time thinking. The villagers all thought he had been afflicted by some strange malady. And at first they made fun of him. Then, they noticed that he was getting thin because he wasn't eating as much as he had been. But he assured them he was fine. And he kept on thinking his problem through.

"When he had outlined exactly the kinds of tools he needed, he began going on long hikes away from the village. It took him fifty hours more to find what he wanted. It was a bed of slate. Slate is a kind of rock, Gigi, that comes in what are called strata. Often, the edges are quite sharp. By rubbing a piece of slate against another kind of rock, he finally shaped both a pickaxe and a spade. Then he got some branches and scraped and shaped them into handles. And at long last he managed to bind the handles to his pieces of slate. He had invented the first pickaxe and the first shovel.

"Now the total amount of time he had expended in making his inventions was three hundred hours, plus the first fifty spent in thinking and the second fifty spent in foraging. So, that meant a grand total of four hundred hours. And by this time, many months had passed and the inventor was terribly skinny and his clothes were in rags.

"But he was now terribly excited about what he was doing. He was like a man possessed. The very next morning he climbed the hill early and began to work. The ground was hard and rocky, and it took a number of days before he had the channel excavated. And by the time he was ready to stop up the flow and get the stream to run the other way, another one hundred hours had gone by. So he had spent five hundred hours altogether.

"Everything worked as he had hoped. And after pausing to pray to the gods that they would not be angry with him for interfering, he put the last rock and the last branches and mud into place in his dam. The water stopped flowing down the ocean face of the hill. It deepened. Then it found the channel he had dug. The water worked its way through that and suddenly began running down the hill toward the village, just as he had intended!

"It was a moment of triumph. He rushed down the hill and called all the villagers together. And here is what he said:

" 'Fellow villagers, I have provided you with a water

supply. Heretofore, each of us had to climb the hill and spend two hours every day getting water. Now, thanks to my inventions of the pickaxe and shovel and thanks to the hard work I have put in, I have brought water right to the village.

" 'So here is my proposition to you. I will let any of you who wish to do so, take water out of the stream right here in the village. If you do so, you will owe me ten minutes each day you help yourself to this water.

" 'Of course, you don't have to do so. Any of you who cares to, can still climb the hill each day and bring back his water in the old way. There is as much water at the top of the hill as before. Possibly more. But I am offering each of you a savings in time and energy amounting to one hundred and ten minutes per day. From here on, those who wish to patronize my water department can make that saving. Those of you who don't wish to do so, needn't bother.

" 'You see, I spent a total of five hundred hours getting you this water. As you begin to take it from me, if you do, I will gradually get back my investment and in the end, assuming that you continue to patronize me, I will be a rich man.' "

I paused and stole a glance at Virginia's face. She was intent on the story. I hoped she would be able to see the implications.

"Papa, what happened next?"

"Well, Gigi, I'm not sure. You see, in a sense we still live in that village and the final decision hasn't been made. Before we deal with that question, let me ask you one. Did the inventor harm the village in any way?"

"Of course not. He helped everyone. He was a very generous man."

"Not everyone, Gigi. He only helped those who patronized him. For them he provided a distinct saving."

"Anyone can see that."

"Henry can't. Henry is calling people who do this exploiters."

"It's not the same as what he was thinking about."

"I think it is. Water is a natural resource. Right? And it's scarce and hard to get. The channel that brought the water down the hill is the same as a store where you can buy things. It's a tool. So, although our original Mr. Newton invented the spade and the pick, he also invented the store, the retail establishment. But he didn't know he had done it, it all happened so naturally."

"And a store saves people time and energy—just like Mr. Newton's channel."

"How did he exploit the village?"

"Well, Papa, you said so yourself. He got rich."

"With what?"

"With all the money the people paid him."

"In my story, they had to pay in time rather than money. But you're right. It's the same thing. But even though he got rich, he made all the villagers richer, too. Each of them could now save a hundred and ten minutes every day. That's seven hundred and seventy minutes every week, for each person.

"True, if all of the villagers patronized him, he took in six hundred and thirty minutes every week, plus his own saving of seven hundred and seventy minutes, so he got richer *faster* than the other villagers. But don't forget, if we are to be fair, he ought to be permitted to earn back the five hundred hours he had invested. And that would take some time. Five hundred hours is 30,000 minutes. So it would take him about forty-three weeks to get back his investment without interest. And if there was an interest charged, it could run maybe fifty or sixty weeks. Let's say he got back his investment in a year's time, fifty-two weeks.

"Assuming the project continued and people continued to patronize his water-store, in time he'd become very rich."

"But that's not really the way it works, is it, Papa?"

"Yes, my dear. The story is precise. It illustrates what we call private capitalism. The only way any businessman can make any money is by providing something for his customers that they will willingly buy. Remember, all purchases are voluntary. Just as the villagers in my story didn't *have to* patronize the water-store.

"So every businessman has to begin by figuring out what other people want and then provide it for them with a saving of some kind. There's no law compelling you to buy from a store. Any time you want something, you can go out and make it if you wish. The only reason, for instance, that you bought that ring in a store is because it was the cheapest and best way for you to get a ring. You could, by working years, have finally gotten all the necessary tools and raw materials and made your own ring. But the storekeeper had anticipated that you and others would be willing to buy from him *if* he saved you all that trouble. So he invested a lot of money and got it all together for you so you wouldn't have to do all that work. In doing so, he benefited all his employees and all his customers, and he made something on his investment, too.

"Tell me, hon, where is the exploitation?"

"The way you tell it, Papa, there isn't any. But that can't always be true."

"Gigi, if you'll keep in mind the principles we've been talking about, you'll see that, assuming we have a free market with no outside forces intervening, it will *always* be true. Of course, the fact is we don't have a free market, so there is some exploiting today. But my point still stands. The only reason anyone goes to the store ever is because it saves him something. It saves time, or money; it's convenient, or there's a better selection, or quite a few of those things put together."

"Papa, you make capitalism sound like a good thing."

"Where is it bad, Gigi? Whom does it hurt?"

"Henry said it hurts the poor."

"The villagers were poor, hon. But our Mr. Newton, who not only invented the store but also private capitalism, made all of them richer. *Everyone* was benefited. But only if they *voluntarily* bought his product. So he didn't affect the others. And those that patronized him were richer than they could have been without him."

"Papa, I really do see that. I wonder how I could have let Henry get me all confused."

"We live in a rather confusing world, Gigi, and it's easy to get mixed up."

She stood. "Thank you, Papa. I really do see it this time. Oh, I'm a very lucky girl to have a papa like you."

Suddenly, her arms were around me and I received a hard, wet kiss.

"I'm glad that old Henry is gone," she said. And then she dashed away.

But there was a note in her voice as she said his name. My little girl had been hurt. And she was hiding a part of that hurt. It would take time before the wound would completely heal.

But what about my own wounds? I had experienced her anguish, made doubly painful by the reflection that I might have been a contributing factor. It was all very well to remind myself that this was "puppy love." Virginia was much too young to entertain serious thoughts of marriage. But who says "puppy love" does not contain real emotion? Who says that the young heart cannot be broken? True, broken hearts do mend. But there are scars. The scars of learning.

And there are other scars that teachers carry. I hoped I had given no sign that Virginia's unawareness of my feelings had left me with an ache, a sense of loss. I hoped that she would soon forget it all. For myself, I was sure that I would always remember.

Chapter 10

THE BUCK STARTS HERE

Several days before my birthday, I became aware of an unusual stirring around our house. I was ordered peremptorily to stay out of certain rooms. Special occasions are the acme of every woman's eye and so I made an effort to be more amenable and flexible than usual. Loy and Virginia went so far as to forbid me the use of my own study during the anniversary and I left the house, wondering if a birthday could justify all the dislocation this one seemed to entail.

After a splendid dinner and the usual ritual of cake and candles, I was ceremoniously conducted to my study. On the wall, concealed by a sheet, what appeared to be a large framed picture turned out to be a blackboard. My wife had purchased it and had it installed during my absence. And along with it was Virginia's gift of a box of chalk and a fine eraser.

I was surprised and very pleased. As a teacher, I have grown accustomed to working with a blackboard and I knew it would be useful to me on many occasions. The two conspirators took great delight in my obvious appreciation.

I was particularly gratified when Virginia insisted that I give her another lesson as soon as possible. One of the highest rewards any teacher ever receives is the attention of an eager pupil. It was a moment of fulfillment and happiness for me.

Obediently, at my suggestion, Virginia sat behind my desk facing the resplendent gift while I stood in front of it.

"I think it's time to discuss what is called a business

cycle, Gigi. And this lovely blackboard will help. In fact, I don't know how to explain a business cycle without drawing a model. It's impossible to explain without some kind of visual assistance, at least for me."

"Then you really do like your present?"

"I most assuredly do. And it's a splendid one."

With chalk I drew a large circle.

"Goods, services, and money move as a result of what we call *demand*. You'll remember what we've already talked about in that area. You remember the law of supply and demand, of course."

"Yes, Papa. The ocean."

"Very good. Now, there are four points on this business cycle that concern us. I will arbitrarily place them on this circle. They are the points of *investment*, *production*, *distribution*, and *sales*."

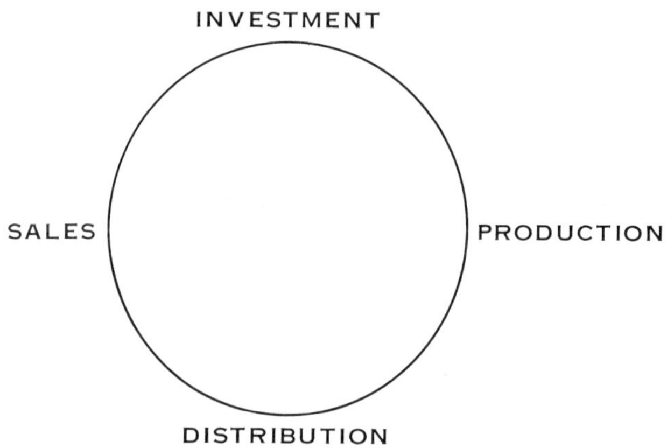

"Let's discuss each one of the points. And we must start with *investment*. This is a very important point. Some economists insist on showing demand as primary and preceding supply, but I prefer to do it this way. Of course, in one sense they are right. The person deciding to make an investment certainly won't do it unless he *believes* there is a demand for what he is going to help provide. But he really doesn't *know*. And as you and I realize, people change their minds all the time and they like things *more* or *less*. Value of anything is never absolute."

"Yes, of course. Like my skirt and the pencils and the money and everything."

"Right. So there isn't any guarantee that the investor is going to provide something people want, at a price they will voluntarily pay. That is why investment is a very risky business. And lots of investors lose their money.

"Let me explain the point I want to make by using a parallel example. Let's suppose you wanted to build a fire. You'd have to have fuel of some kind, and then you'd have to have a match or something to start the fuel burning. Would anything else be necessary?"

She thought about it and then shook her head. "I don't think so. A match and some wood, with maybe some paper to help get it to burn."

"There is something else, Gigi."

"Really? I can't think what it would be."

"Oxygen. Fire won't burn without oxygen."

"Well, that's true, of course. But you always have oxygen."

"No, you don't. If you want a fire in a furnace, for instance, you have to arrange so that a draft of air can get to the spot where combustion occurs. And to prove it, all you have to do is cover a lighted candle with a jar of some sort. The candle will go out at once. It can't burn without oxygen."

"All right. I know that."

"Good. Demand is like oxygen. Remember, we decided that people are *wanters*. They want things all the time. Demand is nearly a constant. It's like oxygen. But demand alone provides nothing. Just as oxygen alone won't provide a fire.

"Now, there are some who imagine that an enlarging population, which will surely increase the amount of demand, will automatically bring about the production of what is needed. But that isn't so. If it were so, those places in the world with the largest populations would have the largest amounts of goods to consume. But think of the huge populations in India and China and Bangladesh. Millions of people. More coming all the time. And a standard of living that is marginal at best and at times so bad that hundreds of thousands die of privation or just plain starve to death.

So, demand isn't a key factor, although it must certainly be present if an investment is to succeed."

"I agree. Still, the investors are pretty smart."

"Not always, hon. Lots of them lose. But the point I want you to grasp is that all business activities begin when somebody makes a decision to *produce something*, and not merely because someone wants something. So investment is primary, and I'm putting it at the top of my circle. I'll move clockwise.

"I'll come back to investment a little later. The next point is *production*. Now, remember the three packages we talked about: natural resources, human energy, and tools? It is at the point of production where these three items come together. The entrepreneur—the man who launches a business or enterprise of some kind—brings together the raw materials, the people, and the tools, including the tool of money, so he can produce the good or service he believes people will buy.

"From here we go to distribution. This is what is called the middle-man. Lots of people think the so-called middle-man takes advantage of producers and customers by charging more than he should. But in fact, all interested in distribution have to be competitive, if we assume a free market—no one interfering with the process. You see, if one distributor began to charge too much, it would be good business for another man to start up to compete with him.

"Distribution, of course, includes transportation; and the costs of moving goods around the country from where they are produced to where they will be purchased by final customers, are enormous. But there's more than that to the job of distributor. In the case of food supplies, for example, he is a processor as well as a mover of goods. At this point on the circle we have packaging, processing, transportation, the maintenance of inventories, storage, and so on. The distributor is taking a big chance, just as everyone does in the market. And a lot of distributors go broke. You see, in order for him to have customers, customers we call retailers, he has to buy in large quantities and pass that saving along to the retailer. Otherwise, the customer would get tired of paying such a high price and would go directly to the producer. Sometimes, when a distributor or wholesaler buys too much of something, he has to store it. Then, right in the midst of everything, people stop buying that particular item. And he's stuck with a warehouse full of goods that people don't want. It happens all the time. So, like everything else, it's a risky business.

"From here, we move to *sales*, which are the function of the retailer. The storekeepers are the retailers who purchase from wholesalers. Then they advertise and try to encourage customers to buy what they have in stock and on display."

My model now looked like this:

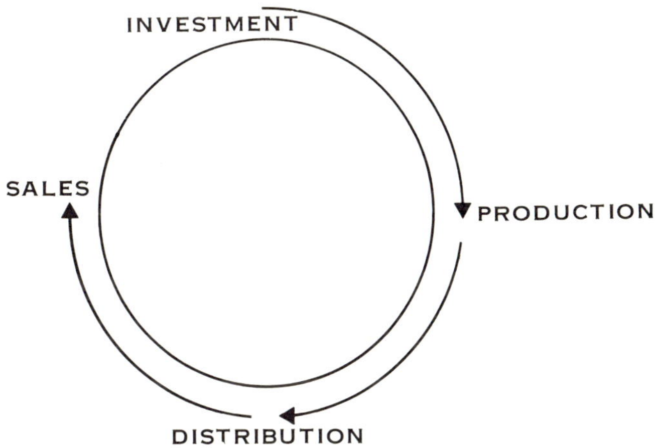

"At this point, the customers, you and I, enter the picture. And in a modern market we bring money with us. And we buy the goods or services the retailer offers. When we do, the money flows in a direction opposite from the flow of goods and services. Some of it is retained by the retailer to pay his costs and to make him a living. And to pay the wages of those who work with him. All the rest of the money then flows to the point of distribution to reward the wholesaler for his costs and his services. Next, the money that is left flows back to the point of production. There, the producer and all his workers are paid, and all the other costs of production are covered. And finally, if anything is left, it flows back up to reward the investor for having made the whole thing possible. That's the way it works."

My model now looked like this:

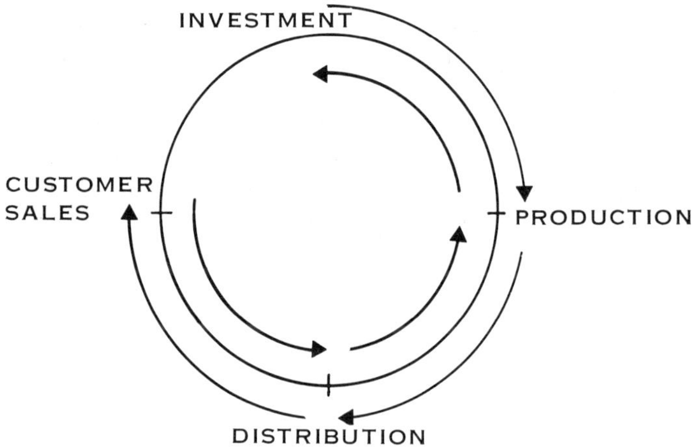

"You'll notice that I've drawn no arrows between customer-sales and investment. That part of the circle is blank. And the reason is pretty clear. Before the investor puts up the money, he first assures himself that production will occur. Before the producer decides to provide the product or service, he makes certain that distribution will occur. And of course, no one becomes a distributor until he assures himself that there are retail outlets that will handle what he proposes to supply. So there is a natural link-up from investment to sales. Indeed, the investor is really looking all the way through the process and anticipates sales or he wouldn't invest at all.

"Now, of course he can't guarantee sales. People don't have to buy what he provides. That's up to them. But why does he make his investment? No one has to make it at all. Why does anyone invest?"

"To provide what we want."

"Hopefully, yes. But why should a man risk his money? Lots of money is lost this way."

"I really don't know."

"Sure, you do, Gigi. Remember, we talked about plus factors. Every action in the market — or outside of it, for that matter — is motivated by what I call plus factors, the hope of gain. The investor, just like every worker and every producer, distributor, or salesman, hopes to gain something as a result of his time and energy and money."

"Of course. I see that."

"Now, anyone can invest. A customer can, or a retailer, a distributor, a producer — or an investor can reinvest. But he isn't going to do it unless he can make something by doing it."

"I can see that."

"Of course. So the one thing that causes anyone to invest is a hope, a belief, that he'll be better off later on because he invested, than he would be if he didn't. I said I'd get back to investment again, and here I am.

"Keep in mind the point I've already made. Nobody gets anything to eat or wear or use, until an investment is made. Investments create all the tools and all the jobs. There aren't any jobs without tools. And there aren't any tools without investment. Now, where do investments come from?"

"From money."

"Sure. But all investments come from *savings*. If everybody took all the money they earned and spent it on things for themselves, there wouldn't by any money available with which to make investments. Remember my story of our Mr. Newton who lived at the bottom of the hill. He made an investment in the expenditure of time and energy before he could provide a water supply to the village. Instead of doing that, he could have continued to fish and hunt with the rest of the villagers. But he conserved his energy and then expended it on an investment. And he got pretty thin and shabby while he was doing it.

"That's what lots of people do, Gigi. They scrimp and save and put money aside. They could have used it up and probably it would have been easier. But they went without things now, so they could have more later on. That's what savings are all about. And without savings, there would be no investments. And without the investments, no tools. Without the tools, no jobs. It's an endless circle, each part fitting into the other parts."

"I see that." I could tell by her expression that she did.

"Now, Gigi, the principal reason we have done so very well in this country relates to the fact that for many years investors had a pretty free hand. They weren't regulated and taxed the way they are now. And that gave incentives to a great many people. The fact that some investments succeeded encouraged other people to make them — all in hopes of plus factors, of making things better later on.

"Unfortunately, today, we are bad-mouthing investors. We read about it and hear about it all the time. We are told that the 'rich guys' are the ones who live on their investments, and many view that as bad. So constant efforts are made to tax investors, and the other productive people, too."

"Well, gosh, Papa. They have so much. And there are so many people who have practically nothing."

"True. But this is not the way to be really helpful. You see, Gigi, no businessman ever really pays a tax. If you *really* tax and regulate him, he goes out of business. If he stays in business but is taxed, he simply passes the cost of taxation along to his customers. And in the end, the final customer is you and I. We pay *all* the taxes for all the businessmen.

"Then why are they always talking about taxing the rich?"

"Because it sounds good, Gigi. People often are very envious of those who do better than they do. So they become selfish in a bad sense. They try to live at the expense of others. Now, if you really want to help the poor, what has to occur is an increase in production at lower and lower costs.

"But that means that we must have more investments so there can be more tools and more jobs. That way, more and more people can get paid for working, not from taking from others against their will. If we increase the numbers of tools, more people can work and be paid. There will be more goods. What happens where there are more goods? Remember supply and demand."

"Of course. Demand goes down."

"That's a good answer, Gigi. That relates to what I've already explained. As more people are able to satisfy their wants from a larger supply of goods, the demand goes down. But in addition, as the supply of goods increases, the prices for those goods decline. So more people can buy more for less money. And that's what we want to see.

"So, if you want to be truly generous, you will figurc out how to save your money and how to invest it. It is one of the most generous things you can do. In fact, I would call making an investment an act of economic virtue."

"Papa, you make it sound so good."

"It is good, Gigi, if we have a free market. We should have as few taxes as possible. Keep in mind, the rich don't pay them, the poor always pay. And they are the least able to pay. And if you plug up the loophole so the businessman has to pay without passing along the added cost, you'll find that he'll just go out of business.

"Now, when you bear in mind that all goods and services are scarce and that the big job is to provide more and more at lower and lower costs, what is the advantage of raising costs?"

"I don't see any."

"Good. Every tax increases the cost that all of us have to meet. So the fewer taxes, the better. That means the lower the costs, the better."

"I can see that."

"True economic virtue means that you make the best possible use of your money. And investment does a great deal more good than welfare. Investments mean more production of the things people want. Welfare means more money in circulation to buy the same amount of goods.

"There are several reasons for that. Keep in mind how our sense of value works. We value most the things that are hard to get or are scarce. When money is made plentiful and is given to people who are not working, it is certainly intended as a kindness. But it causes those people to value money less than they would if they had to earn it. They are led to believe they can always get money by not working. And if that becomes true, they won't produce anything yet they are able to go into the store and effectively demand what others have produced.

"Wouldn't it be better to help provide the tools so they could earn their own money—good-selfish—rather than living at the expense of others—bad-selfish?"

"Sure, it would, Papa. But what about the people who are old or sick and can't work?"

"Obviously, Gigi, that is a problem. And we are

naturally concerned about others because it makes us feel good when we are. And may I say that all of us, one time or another, will probably be down on his luck and need a helping hand. Sure. That happens, and we need to have a way of solving that problem.

"But any kind of a regular handout which can be had for not working, becomes destructive. Other things happen, too, which I hope we'll get to at a later time. So, if we are really kind, we won't let people become dependent on charity if we can possibly help it. Sure, we can be kind. It's important. But kindness means helping another to produce, not helping another to become a parasite. That isn't kindness at all. Not really.

"Let's suppose that the government paid everyone a salary if he lost his job. And let's suppose that the salary was almost as large as what he would get if he worked. What do you think people would do?"

"Why, they'd stop work, of course. Why would anyone work hard if he could make nearly as much if he didn't work?"

"Correct. And that means that more and more people would manage to lose their jobs so they could be gainfully unemployed. It would be a gain for them. But with the passing of time, fewer and fewer people would be working and more and more people would be living at their expense. If you carry it out, finally no one would work, but all of us would be paid. What then?"

"Why, nothing would be produced."

"Right. And then what could we buy with our money if there were no stores and no factories and nothing being produced?"

"Gosh, Papa."

"What is it, hon?"

"That's what Henry wanted to see. He said the government ought to pay us all whether we worked or not."

"How do you think it would work out?"

"Now that you've explained it, it wouldn't work out at all. It'd be terrible!"

"It sure would be."

I put down my chalk and left the model on the board. She was staring at it and I could almost hear the wheels in her head turning.

"Thanks again for this beautiful birthday present, Gigi. I like it a lot."

She continued to sit at my desk, so I quietly left the room.

Chapter 11

HONESTY AND PRIVACY

Virginia spent the summer months away from our home. When she rejoined our household a week before school began, I hardly knew her. She had grown at least an inch, and her slender boyish figure was beginning to fill out. She was thirteen.

The first time she came into my study after her return, she walked with her head high and with her face displaying studied maturity and the experience of a woman of thirty. Her hair had been swept up to the top of her head in a braided coil. The unruly locks that I had loved to run my fingers over were under harsh discipline. I thought I detected the texture of face powder and perhaps a trace of rouge. If present, it was only a trace.

Despite the care she had taken with face and hair, her attire was conspicuous for non-care. She wore faded blue denims with frayed trouser cuffs and an attention-getting array of watermarks. Her shirt tail flapped in the rear and the shirt buttons had been left open three-quarters of the way to her belt line. I'm afraid my eyebrows arched when through the gap I caught sight of a curved breast and at the same time took note of the sensuous way she now filled out her trouser legs. Virginia was growing up.

She stopped before my desk, her legs spread wide, her torso leaning to windward, exactly as fashion models disport themselves.

"Hello," she said. There was a "come hither" look in her eyes. I wasn't certain Virginia knew it was there.

"Hello," I responded. She had obviously learned a great

deal during the summer. She had my attention and was conscious of resources by means of which she could obtain still more.

"You're getting to be quite a woman," I said.

"I hope so." Her eyes were only partly open. One hand strayed to her gapping shirt front and played with the unpressed muslin. Clearly, Virginia was putting on an act for my benefit. She was too reserved, too basically shy, to conduct herself in such a manner in front of any stranger.

"Are you trying to seduce me?" I asked.

She looked startled. "Why, what a thing to say!" She undulated with staged serpentine grace, and a hint of color spread upward from her slender throat.

"Whether you intend to or not, you're doing all the right things." I smiled at her. "Virginia, we missed you. The house seemed empty. It's good to have you back."

She tossed her head and permitted her eyes to slowly open wide. "We? I was hoping you'd say that *you* missed me."

I grinned. "I did, my dear. So did Loy. Tell me about your summer. Did you have a good time?"

She shrugged. "Oh, it was all right. I met a few people. Did a couple of things. You know."

"I don't really know."

"Sure, you do." She put her hands on my desk and leaned toward me, her lips open slightly. "It's really super being back with *you* again."

I leaned back in my chair, holding my eyes on her face with some effort. "And it's super having you here. If you want to talk with me, why don't you get a chair and sit down? Towering over me this way is rather intimidating."

She giggled. "I just had to do it. I just had to do it! Trudy said it would, and it does! Wow, man!"

"Who is Trudy and what would do what it does?"

"Oh, Trudy is a girl. You know."

"Gigi, you are beginning to confuse me."

"Am I really? Oh, that's wonderful. Men *are* all alike, aren't they?"

"I suppose so. In some ways. In other ways, each of us is unique. Remember any of the things I talked to you about? I mean about economics?"

"Of course I do." She paused and then blurted, "I've

got a favor to ask."

"Ask away."

"Promise you'll do as I ask."

"Certainly not, young lady. Not until I hear what the favor is. You know I'll do it if I can."

"I'll consider that a promise. All right, then. Do you mind if I call you Bob?"

I was startled. "No, I guess not. I rather do like being called 'Papa,' though."

"That's silly," she said archly. "You are not my papa. You're my very special friend. You call me by *my* first name. I should think you'd want me to call you by *your* first name. Loy does."

I nodded. "So she does. It's all right with me if you prefer it that way."

"Well, I'm certainly not going to call you by your last name. That would be too formal."

"I agree."

"Then you don't mind?"

"Not really, I guess."

She squealed in delight. "Oh, thank you, Papa." She darted around the desk, threw her arms about my neck, and aimed a kiss at my mouth. I turned in time and was rewarded with warm moisture on the cheek.

She drew back. "Don't you want me to kiss you any more?"

"I certainly hope that you will kiss me when a show of affection is in order. If, however, your objective is to kiss and to be kissed, I am a little old and already spoken for."

"Oh, that! People aren't that way any more, Pa. . . Bob. You have to get with it. I told Trudy you were real mod. I hope I wasn't wrong."

"I hope so, too. I suspect I'm mod enough."

"Now that I'm grown up, I think you and I should treat each other as equals, not as adult-child any more."

"In that case, Gigi, get the chair and let's talk like adults."

"Please, . . . uh, Bob."

"Please what?"

"Not that any more. Not *Gigi!* That's for a child. You can certainly call me Virginia."

"Yes, I certainly can. I can also think of a number of other things I could call you. Gigi was my term of affection for you. You have had a very special place in my heart, my dear."

"Of course. Don't you think *I* know *that?* You love me, don't you, Bob?"

"Certainly, I do. Very much."

"Well, then!"

She marched away and came back with the chair, which she shoved against my desk chair so firmly it would no longer swivel. She plopped down in it and leaned against me. "You see, Papa, people don't keep things to themselves any more. If a certain person loves a certain person, they say so. It's old-fashioned to bottle up your emotions. Today, everybody lets it all hang out. See what I mean?"

"I would have to be deaf, dumb, and blind not to get your implication."

"Oh, we're going to have some wonderful times together, you and me," she said. "When I think of the opportunities I had with you last year and just let them slip through my fingers! Boy, *that* won't happen again, I can tell you."

"Opportunities?"

"Sure. You know. Like the time we went to the beach. And the time we went for that drive up Mulholland."

"Yes, I saw those excursions as opportunities myself. But I had the notion, doubtless an old-fashioned one, that we took full advantage of the opportunities to expand your knowledge in the field of economics."

"Oh, you are a dear, silly man," she said. "You know, you really are sweet."

"Very well," I said. "I'll file those compliments away for future reference. I'm 'dear, silly, and sweet.' What I want to know right now is how much of the economic lessons I taught you last year you still remember."

"Why, I remember it all, Bob. Every tiny bit. I haven't forgotten a single thing. Not one thing."

"Splendid. Are you ready for another lesson?"

"Is there more?"

I looked at her, showing my surprise. "You didn't think I had explained everything about economics, did you?"

"Well, of course. It all made sense. I can put all the

pieces together now."

"All of them?"

"Why, of course!" She laughed. "I guess you just don't realize what a fantastic teacher you really are."

"I'm beginning to have grave doubts about my ability to teach anything."

"You're teasing."

"Indeed, I'm not. For example, there seems to be one thing I do remember saying that you've forgotten. I told you I was an ignorant man. I don't know everything."

"Well, you do, too. About economics."

"No, my dear. Not even about economics. So if you can put *all* the pieces together, you know more about it than I do. Perhaps we'd best reverse our roles, now that you are an adult. Perhaps you'd best teach me and bring me up to date."

She took it seriously. "Well, *that's* true. You *are* a little old-fashioned. I know. I can bring you up to date and you can tell me any little point you think I may have missed."

"All right," I agreed. "That seems fair."

"I remember about that!" she chortled. "About all you said about being fair. And you're right. I was able to explain gobs and gobs of things to Trudy. I really helped her a lot. It's really important to know those things."

"Good. And I now realize one very big item I didn't cover at all. Do you remember the little story I told you about our Mr. Newton?"

"Mr. Newton?" She frowned, then clapped her hands. "Oh, yes. I do remember. The man who lived in the tribe near the hill and who invented tools and water conservation and a free market."

"Virginia, he invented *certain* tools, not all of them. Remember, when he lived, pails and huts and quite a few other things had already been invented. He just worked out the spade and the pickaxe and sort of invented the store, the retail establishment. But there was something else he did that I didn't dwell on."

"Oh?" Her nose crinkled. "What?"

"He invented privacy."

"Privacy? You didn't say anything about that."

"I know it. I see now that I should have done so.

Remember how long our Mr. Newton worked just thinking through his problem? And then how he went off alone in the forest and through the savannahs trying to find what he wanted. And all the other things he did.

"Well, my dear, during that whole time he told no one at all about what he was planning to do. He kept it all to himself.

"Now, I must let you in on a little secret. Mr. Newton was the first man who kept a secret. Prior to that time, everyone in every tribe did everything right out in front of everyone else."

"Everything?" Virginia giggled. "You don't mean *everything?*"

"Oh, but I do."

"That couldn't be, Papa."

"Why not?"

"Well, people don't go to the bathroom in public, for goodness sake."

"Not any more, Virginia. But they used to."

"They did?"

"Of course. In fact, until quite recent times, going to the bathroom publicly was a common practice in many European countries and certainly this was true in other places, too. When I was in Paris, public toilets accommodated both men and women. And that was only a few years ago, really, during World War II. You went down a flight of steps and a woman at the bottom, a kind of concierge, collected a couple of francs' admission. If you were a lady, you turned left; if a man, you turned right. The stools lined both far walls and there weren't even any swinging doors in place. You simply sat there with your britches down and looked across the room directly at members of the opposite sex engaged in the same thing you were doing."

Virginia clapped both hands to her mouth and stared at me, her eyes round.

"Oh, Papa. Why, that's terrible! I couldn't do a thing like that. Why, that's terrible!"

"I'm on your side, hon. In fact, after I'd paid my two francs I found that I couldn't perform at all. I just wasted two francs. But lots of people didn't mind and still don't."

"Papa, that's disgusting."

"All right, Virginia. We needn't dwell on it. I simply wanted you to know that similar practices occur everywhere. And keep in mind that the French are a fine, upright, highly skilled, very sensitive and cultivated people. Of course, the French believe in and practice privacy very well. In other respects. It was just that in this case, they didn't think that privacy mattered.

"Well, our Mr. Newton was the first man who decided to keep his mouth closed about what he was thinking. You see, he wasn't certain how his inventions would work. He really wasn't sure about anything. So he figured that if he talked about what he proposed doing, people would begin arguing with him and they might get angry with him and maybe prevent him from going ahead. So he shut up.

"Of course, like the rest of the people of his tribe, he went to the bathroom in public and thought nothing of it. He dressed and undressed the same way. Everybody did. They sort of 'let it all hang out,' as you say. Of course, that wasn't 'mod' at all. It's very, very old-fashioned."

Virginia sat very straight in her chair and looked at me with puzzlement. I ignored the look and continued.

"You see, Virginia, all economic study is about human action. If a person had to take everyone into his confidence every time he wanted to invent something or wanted to dispose of a property in a certain way and for a certain purpose, very little would get done.

"I'm sure you've run into this sort of thing at school. When you tell people about a new idea you have, the first thing most of them do is pooh-pooh it. They tell you that you're crazy, that it can't be done, that what you do will upset others. People are like that. It's probably a part of the tendency many have to convert competition into conflict.

"Perhaps at school you've already studied about Galileo and Copernicus. After he invented a telescope, Galileo learned that planets rotate about the sun. Now, when he was working on his telescope, if he had explained to very many others what he was doing, they'd have been on his neck like a herd of buffalo. As it was, when he finally did reveal what his telescope proved, he was taken before a high tribunal and forced to retract what he had discovered.

People simply couldn't stand the truth that he had found. If he hadn't been secretive about it, the telescope might never have been invented.

"And Copernicus learned that the earth is not the center of our solar system. He was well enough informed about human nature so that he didn't even reveal his truth until on his death bed. And then people sought to burn him for heresy. The popular view at the time, sustained by the organized church and the forces of government, was that the earth was the center of the universe. If Copernicus hadn't practiced privacy, none of us might ever have learned the real nature of the universe.

"Actually, what we call civilization is a movement in the direction of privacy. The more we are allowed to mind our own business and keep our own counsel, the better off we will be. I'm speaking about economic reality, of course.

"That is what our Mr. Newton discovered. He sort of instinctively knew that when you 'let it all hang out,' people can and sometimes will take advantage of you or put blocks in your road. It is far wiser and far more modern to manage your own affairs."

Virginia began shaking her head slowly. "Oh, Papa. That's so *different*. Trudy was saying that it was secrecy that hurt everyone *psychologically*. It's bad for people to bottle up their emotions. We're supposed to tell everyone *everything*. Because, when you do, you're *honest*. And you're *fair*. You're not hiding anything. It's hiding and being furtive and secretive that is so bad!"

"My dear girl. This is a very important distinction to make, but we must make it. To be honest doesn't mean that you have to tell everything. What it means is that you must not tell a lie. It's perfectly honest to keep a secret and to mind your own business. Like the time you auctioned off your dress last year. Remember? If you had told everyone what you were up to, you'd have made lots of people angry with you. Yet you did nothing wrong. In fact, you helped a great many people, as we learned. And you helped yourself, too.

"You and Trudy don't know anything about this from personal experience, of course, but when I was your age there was no income tax in this country to amount to anything. The result was that a man's income was his own business. Nobody could find out what a person made unless the individual chose to reveal it himself.

"Do you think that was bad for us? I'll tell you what it meant. It meant that a man could take pride in his work and not merely in his income. He didn't have to tell anyone how many dollars he earned. We produced and were paid for what we produced.

"Now, here's what has happened. As the government began taxing us in our incomes, all of us were forced to report what our dollar-take was. The immediate result was jealousy. We found out that some people made more than we did. And it is human nature to resent that and to demand that we get as much for our work as the next person.

"What happened after that? Why, people got organized into all kinds of groups and began to get laws passed to regulate wages and to try to divide up the earnings evenly. Instead of seeing that fairness is the opportunity to do your best as a person, most people began to think of fairness as an equal supply of dollars. Or an equal supply of land. Or an equal supply of food, clothing, or shelter.

"And I think you do remember your lessons about that, don't you?"

Virginia nodded mutely. She looked as though she wanted to say something so I waited. Finally, in a small voice she said, "Why did the government do that?"

"Because it wanted to do good, Virginia. The people in government wanted to be helpful. All of us usually find real pleasure in helping others, and politicians are no exception. Indeed, they make careers out of appearing publicly as champions of help to everyone. They had good intentions, I'm sure. Or at least we can assume that most of them did.

"It's just that reality isn't that way. And as we know, in the end, reality rules. So we have to keep in mind that being honest isn't the same thing as 'letting it all hang out.' And being fair doesn't mean an equal distribution of the prizes; it means the opportunity each person does have unless he is interfered with, of doing his very best."

We sat quite still for some minutes.

"Papa, why am I so dumb?"

"Why, hon, you're not at all dumb. Quite the reverse."

"But you really did explain all this before."

"I did and I didn't. I don't think I once mentioned privacy. You see, my dear, the long march humankind has taken has been a movement away from the idea of collectivity toward the idea of privacy. We can talk about this some more if you wish. But I think you've gotten quite a bundle of information in your pretty head right now."

"Thank you." She stood. Then she reached for my right hand and gave it a single shake and a squeeze. "Thank you, Bob. I hope you still like me."

I smiled. There was nothing that had to be said.

She straightened and walked away in dignity.

Chapter 12

LEAVE ME ALONE

Household relationships for the next two weeks appeared to be stable. Gradually it dawned on me that Virginia's attitude had undergone a subtle change. She talked to Loy a good deal but was only marginally interested in any economic point I advanced. When I unintentionally overheard one of their conversations, I discovered that it was mere surface chatter. But I was busy and accepted as unavoidable the emergence of shallow discussion as a counterpoint to what otherwise filled a probing and penetrating young mind.

And then I awoke one day with a sinking feeling. The avoidance of serious discussion plus the light and aimless chatter were parts of a well-conceived program. Virginia had decided to keep things to herself.

I was hurt. She had been so open and confiding, it had helped to create a relationship that was very flattering and fulfilling. I had felt needed and useful. Now I was bypassed. Suddenly, I was someone Virginia tried to avoid.

My first impulse was to insist on a frank discussion to see if the former relationship could be re-established. However, I recalled my last conversation and realized that Virginia was acting out my own advice. I had insisted, with quite other ends in view, that she learn to mind her own business and that keeping things to herself was not dishonest or wrong. It hadn't occurred to me that she would apply that lesson in this particular way.

One afternoon I thought I heard footsteps outside my study and concluded that Virginia had come from school.

Finishing my work, I thought I'd pass the time of day with her, doubtless hoping subconsciously that she'd find my presence agreeable. I went to her room, knocked, and, getting no answer, opened the door.

She was not to be seen. However, I detected a strange odor. Odd that she would be attracted to that scent as a perfume. I wondered where she got it. Then I froze in alarm. What I smelled wasn't perfume, it was perfumed cigarette smoke. Someone had been smoking in her bedroom.

Loy didn't smoke. And unless there was an alien intruder, Virginia was the smoker.

That evening at dinner Virginia was quite communicative, shutting me out and concentrating on girl talk with my wife. I decided to become a party to the conversation unless a very firm and personal rebuff prevented it.

"It occurs to me, Virginia," I said, "that you haven't told us anything about Trudy. You mentioned her as someone you met this summer. Is she attending school with you or did you meet her somewhere else?"

She looked at me blankly. "Trudy? What Trudy?"

"I have no idea what Trudy. You mentioned her just after you got back from your vacation."

"I did?" She shook her head. "I don't know any Trudy."

"Perhaps I imagined it. I thought it was someone you met this summer."

Remembrance came back. "Oh, *her*. *That* Trudy. Oh, sure. What about her?"

"I just wondered if you were seeing her a great deal these days."

"Good heavens, no. She's someone I met at camp, that's all. I haven't seen her in years."

"Trudy and I seem to be in the same category," I said.

She frowned. "What is that supposed to mean?"

"We both seem to be people you used to know. Years ago, of course."

"I don't know what you mean. I certainly have an ongoing relationship with you. I know you *very* well. Very well, indeed."

Implications bristled from her tone, although the words were innocent enough.

"I'm glad to know that you and I have an on-going relationship. I had begun to feel like an outsider."

"Oh, no, Bob. You aren't an outsider. Most definitely not." She gave me a look of patent insincerity. "I have learned a great many things from you."

"I hope what I have told you has been useful, Virginia. I just thought you'd like to confide in me a little more. Who are you palling around with these days? Is there another young man with some of the fine qualities Henry had? Are you and Mabel good friends now?"

"Mabel? No, she graduated. I haven't seen her for a long time."

"Is there another young man, Virginia?"

"No. Not at all."

She wasn't volunteering anything. "Hon, I guess it's none of my business but I am interested. Who are your girl friends right now? If I'm prying, tell me so and I'll forget it."

"Well, you ought to know. You made me go with her."

"I did? Who in the world are you talking about?"

"You know very well."

"I'm sure I ought to know, but I really don't. I don't recall making you pal around with anyone."

"You did so, Bob. You certainly have a big forgettery, don't you? Helen, of course."

"Helen?"

"The rich girl. The one who bought my skirt. You said I shouldn't let all her money interfere with my liking her. So I like her now. Satisfied?"

"Oh. Helen." I nodded as though I understood. "What kind of a girl is she?"

"What kind of girls are there, Bob? We're all alike, aren't we? She has two legs and two arms and a head. She's a little thin but quite pretty when you get used to her. And she has a younger brother named Harvey. And if you think I'm interested in him, well, you're wrong. He's a mere child, a freshman. But Helen and Harvey and me, and a few others, do lots and lots of things together."

"Is it some kind of club?"

"Of course not. Who wants an old club, anyhow?"

"I'm sure I wouldn't know."

"Then why are you asking all these dumb questions?" Hostility darkened her face.

"All right, Virginia. I have been beating around the bush. I went into your room shortly before dinner. I thought I detected some kind of cigarette smoke. Have you decided to take up smoking?"

Virginia gripped her fork convulsively. Then she carefully laid it on her plate. "It's none of your business."

"Really? How do you figure that?"

"Well, I'm just following out your instructions. You told me it was a good thing to mind my own business. And I'm doing it. But you aren't. You're poking and prodding into my affairs and I don't like it."

"Please don't be angry, Virginia. Maybe you're right. Perhaps I shouldn't be asking these questions. Put it down as the nosiness of someone who is more than a little bit interested in you. As you know, I smoke a pipe. It occurred to me that if you really want to smoke, I could get you a pipe and then you and I could smoke together. It would be something we shared, something we had in common."

Virginia stared at me, disbelief on her face. "You don't want me to smoke, do you?"

"Did I say that? I don't remember saying it. What I'm getting at is the feeling of separation I've been experiencing. You've virtually shut me out of your life. And that makes me lonely. I feel abandoned. And if it's just the smoking that's doing it, then perhaps we could learn to smoke together. Perhaps I could get a pipe for Loy, too, and all three of us can smoke."

A smile was twitching her lips. "Bob, I *can't* smoke a pipe."

"Why not? Have you got a prejudice?"

"Girls don't smoke pipes."

"You mean girls are chauvinists? I thought girls and boys were supposed to be able to do the same things. Let me put it this way, hon. If you want to smoke, I would much prefer to have you smoke openly. I'd hate to feel that you had to sneak off to indulge yourself."

"Ha!" She crumpled her napkin and put it on the table. "That's not what you said before. You distinctly told me that I was to learn to mind my own business. I don't have to tell you what I'm doing or why. I'm being fair. I'm not telling *you* what you have to do. Why do you insist on telling *me* what I have to do?"

Loy and I exchanged glances and she began clearing the table. The look on her face showed me that Virginia had an ally. I had apparently been caught in an inconsistency.

"First, Virginia, I'm not telling you what you have to do. I'm sure you've heard all the arguments about tobacco before now. I can tell you, as an habitual user of the weed, that it's a smelly, dirty habit. But you know that, and I certainly am not going to insult your intelligence."

"Well, thank goodness for that." She was somewhat relieved.

"Of course, some of the young people smoke pot — marijuana. Come to think of it, they sometimes do use a pipe, I believe. But I believe marijuana also is available in cigarette form. Are you smoking pot?"

Her eyes flashed fire. "What if I was? I'm not saying I am, but I'm not saying I'm not. What's it to you?"

"Well, there are some economic principles that may apply here and this seems like a good time to spell them out. Let me assure you that I don't intend forbidding you. First, it would do no good. I'm not going to lock you in your room or take any kind of physical measures. So if you really want to smoke, even pot, you'll figure out how to do it. I'm satisfied that you're smart enough and ingenious enough to pretty well do what you please.

"But you and I have a special kind of relationship, Virginia. Let me remind you of something you agreed to some time ago. I explained that you were a guest here in my house. I speak here for Loy as well as for myself. I make the rules respecting my house. So long as you stay here, I will have to insist that you respect my rules. Now, if you are tired of staying here as my guest, just say so and we can make some other arrangements."

"Bob, I'm not hurting you at all. It's none of your business what I do with myself. I own myself. I'm my own person. If I want to smoke or drink or anything else, it's my business."

"True enough. But so long as you do it in my house, it becomes my business, too. So, let's get a couple of points into the record."

I took a deep breath and looked at her closely. The firm ground of our relationship seemed to be washing away. More than ever before, I realized how valuable, how important, how vital Virginia was. At the same time, I could see her problem—the urge to self-mastery, the resentment against the slightest touch of even a kindly hand that might seemingly influence and hence control.

In a quiet voice I said, "One: I love you very much and want you to stay on as my guest.

"Two: I am not angry with you in the least.

"Three: I have great respect for your judgment. I think you are a very bright person and that if you have the facts, you will make reasonably good decisions.

"Four: I am not going to force you to do anything against your will. However, I will insist that you obey my rules so long as you stay in my house, eat my food, and wear the clothing I have provided. Obviously, if you leave, I'll have nothing more to say whatever. Is that all understood?"

"Of course it is." She tossed her head. "So where do you come off giving me a lecture?"

"We haven't had time to talk about property and the meaning of boundaries as yet, Virginia. But I'm sure you do understand it. The owner of something, whether it is a skirt, or a ring or a house, is the one who is to decide about how that property is to be used. Now, I don't own you. You are the one who has to decide about you; about what you will eat or drink or smoke or wear, and so on.

"But we have a kind of contract here. You are my guest. I am putting up the funds so that you eat regularly and have a bed to sleep in and clothes to wear. I'm paying for your books in school and for quite a number of other things. So long as I go on doing those things, you are obligated to follow the rules in respect to those properties I provide.

"A contract, which is what we have, is a kind of property in itself. Just as I don't own you, you don't own me or my house or my money. We have a working arrangement, you and I.

"A contract is like any other form of property. Among

its characteristics it has certain boundaries. For instance, if I failed to provide you with food, I would be in violation of the contract. I am obligated to provide certain things because I assumed that obligation. Paying for your food and for other things costs me quite a bit. Of course, I could find other places to put the money. But obviously, I don't mind in the least. I willingly assumed the obligation; the boundary to this contract.

"The point is: if I didn't provide the food, or anything else that I have agreed to provide, I would have violated a boundary. The effect would be a kind of theft. I would have kept from you something I agreed to provide and which, as a result of that agreement, you had a right to expect. It would be a wrongful act. And neither of us favors stealing, do we, Virginia?"

"Of course not. But it's not the same thing. Stealing means that you take something from someone else. If you *didn't* provide something, it would be the opposite of stealing."

"Let's think about that a little more. Let's suppose I decided to buy a new car and didn't have enough money to pay cash. What would I do?"

"You'd have to borrow the money."

"Right. I'd buy the car by borrowing; probably I'd buy the car on time payments. That would mean that I entered an obligation willingly. The dealer would give me the car on the condition that I agreed to pay for it over a period of time. Now, if I didn't pay for it, I would have violated the agreement. That means I would have obtained a property against the will of the owner. He wanted me to pay, but I didn't."

"But I still don't. . . . "

"Wait a second. Don't go so fast. Why do you think Loy and I agreed to the obligation of having you here with us?"

She started to respond, then clamped her lips shut.

"Have you any idea?"

"It's just that you and Loy are wonderful people, Bob. That's all. You're different from others. Oh, you may not think so, but you really are."

"Wrong. We were seeking a profit."

"A profit? You're making a profit out of me?"

"Of course."

She shook her head. "And I guess I'm just a big fat loss all the way around, huh?"

"Not at all. At least not yet. That's why I'm talking to you. I'm trying to protect my investment, my prospects of making a profit. Let me explain just what kind of profit it is.

"First of all, Virginia, we love you. And having you here as an object of our love is a very profitable thing. That's probably the biggest profit there is. But there's more. We have the profit of seeing you mature; of helping you learn how to handle your affairs, of growing up into a beautiful, understanding woman, capable of making her own way in the world. All of that reflects favorably on us. Think how proud we can be.

"Later on, people will ask: 'Who is this Virginia? She seems like such a wonderful, gracious person.' And then Loy and I can say, 'Virginia? Oh, she's the young lady we helped to raise.' Can you just imagine how we can preen and look satisfied and then accept the congratulations of those we know? Boy, I can just about pop a couple of shirt buttons thinking about how proud I will be. That is, how proud I will be if I fulfill the terms and obligations of our contract and provide you with the food, clothing, shelter, and medical care and whatever else you may need until you are fully mature and on your own.

"Think how badly I'd feel if people were to praise you and then I'd have to hang my head and say, 'Well, I had the opportunity of helping to raise her, but I goofed up. I didn't provide the food or the other things she needed. She succeeded in spite of us. We can take no credit for what she has become.' "

"All right. You don't have to spell it out. You want to mold me. You're trying to exploit me. I'm supposed to do whatever *you* think I should do just to protect your lousy profits. I'm nothing but a piece of furniture to you. So you won't let me smoke or drink or do anything I want to. Otherwise, you'll lose money on me. That's it, isn't it?"

"No, it isn't. Not at all. Let's look at it this way. All relationships are profit-motivated relationships on *both* sides. The only reason you continue to stay here with us is because that is profitable to you. That's really the only reason you're here. When the time comes that it is more profitable for you to be elsewhere, you'll go in a minute. So, what are *you* doing? You're trying to exploit me. You're here just to protect *your* lousy profits. I'm nothing but food and clothing and shelter to you. And that's what you don't want to lose. Right?"

Virginia looked startled. "Why, but . . . no, it isn't like that . . . well . . . yes . . . I see what you mean . . . . Oh, dear! I didn't look at it that way before."

"Virginia, would I be warranted in claiming that you are just trying to get your hands on my income so you can take me for everything you can wheedle out of me?"

"I'm not like that at all. You know that. How can you say such things?"

"Good. Then how can you accuse me of the same thing? It's what you're doing when you say I want to exploit you, or that I'm trying to mold you."

"That's what Helen says. She says that parents just exploit their kids. That they take out their frustrations on their kids and try to put them in a straitjacket so they can't do anything at all. And it's none of the parents' business what the child does. The child is her own person. She owns herself. And what if smoking is bad for me? It's my lungs and it's my body. I have a right to put anything into it I want to."

"Virginia, let's go back and start from the beginning. By our natures, each of us wants plus factors. Each of us is egocentric; self-interested. You want your relationships to be profitable to you. I want mine to be profitable to me. Up until now, the relationship between us was mutually profitable. That's what has been so great about it. And of course you've understood it. You're an extremely smart young lady. You found out a long time ago that by being considerate of us and by doing the things you were asked to do, you were rewarded. That was your way of investing in our relationship.

"Both Loy and I then did our best so that you got a dividend in return for desirable behavior. We gave you gifts; we brought you into our discussions; we planned special outings with you. You became a partner in everything we did. A very important partner.

"What have I been doing to try to earn a dividend on my investment? I've been trying to show you the difference between right and wrong. I've been trying to have you glimpse the nature of reality and to help you see things the way they really are. Why? Because I want you to emerge as the kind of person Loy and I can be proud of. I want a favorable reflection from you later on. That's my long-term profit. My dividend from you is your love and trust.

"Helen and many other people may think that by seeking to direct and reward you, I'm trying to *mold* you, trying to put you into a straitjacket. If I were, Virginia, do you think I would be so insistent upon the necessity of having you make up *your* own mind? If I really wanted to mold you, I'd make the decisions for you and insist on obedience. Instead, I do my best to show you the true nature of life and the true nature of the world we are in. Naturally, I hope that you'll make wise decisions. But wise or foolish, I let you make them. That is, I let you make them in respect to your own life and property. And you're quite right. Your body is yours. And you have a right to do as you please with it. You also have the right to jump off a cliff if you wish.

"Now, if you came in here and told me that you had decided to jump off a cliff, would I be exploiting you and trying to put you in a straitjacket if I said to you, 'Okay, hon. Jump off the cliff if you insist. However, I hope you won't because it will probably injure you if it doesn't kill you.' "

"Smoking isn't the same as jumping off a cliff."

"Of course it isn't. But bear in mind, I haven't told you not to smoke and I'm not going to tell you that. I have faith in your good judgment. But look at it through my eyes for a moment. Will a negative act enhance my investment? You know that it won't. But I'm not going to pretend with you, Gigi — I don't approve of your smoking, especially the way you are going about it. But I won't forbid it. And I won't approve of your jumping off a cliff, and for the same reason. But again, I won't forbid it.

"You see, all you'd be doing in either case would be running up my costs, or potential costs, and at the same time downgrading my chances for profit. And I have a right to look out for my own interests to see that I'm not exploited, just as you have a right to look out for your own interests to see that you're not exploited."

"If I smoke, it'll be at *my* expense. It won't cost you a thing."

"Oh? I thought we already understood that. I give you an allowance. And there is a limited number of scarce dollars. Either you will spend some of your own money for cigarettes, or you'll have to cadge them from others. If you spend some of your money that way, you won't have the same amount of money to buy other things. That means you'll either go without the other things or I'll have to increase your allowance to keep you at the same level. You know that. There's no magic to it. There's just so much when it comes to all scarce resources, including money.

"But this isn't quite fair because money isn't really that important to either of us. I've mentioned it because we often tend to think in terms of money. My real investment in you, Gigi, is in love. And I think that is the nature of your investment in this same partnership we have. So my real hang-up here isn't that you decided to smoke. It's that you decided to smoke *secretly*, obviously believing that I would interfere and impose on you. And that is a little hard to take.

"Now, it's at this point that I feel that my investment is threatened. It's my investment in love and understanding, not my outlay of money. By becoming secretive, you have shut me out of your life. I think we have a very wonderful and profitable relationship in being able to share one another's confidence."

Virginia pushed back from the table and paced the room in agitation.

"You're not being consistent." She hurled the phrase at me accusingly. "No, you're not! I felt all warm and cozy toward you. I thought how great we were; so very special. With each other, I mean. And *you* shut *me* out. You told me to mind my own business! Well, all right, Mister 'Know-it-all,' how do you like it? I'm minding my own business and now *you* feel all shut out and hurt. Well, I'm glad. Now you know how it feels!"

I gulped and gripped the arms of my chair.

"Whoa! Wait a minute. Gigi, you have a way of reading more into what I say than I implied. All right. Perhaps I didn't put it the best way. Think back. I didn't tell you to mind your own business. I told you that it isn't wrong to have a secret; that what is wrong is to tell a lie. If I made you feel that I was shutting you out, then I helped cause something I don't want at all.

"Virginia, it isn't wrong to share things with others. It isn't wrong to perform even very private acts in front of those who love you. I was also trying to explain that it isn't wrong to keep things to yourself, if you care to.

"What I was trying to offset in your mind was the view that so many have; the view that keeping a secret is dishonest. It certainly is not. However, sharing something with another isn't dishonest, either. *You* have to decide. Obviously, when people live together in the same house and share the same income and the same food, they become very close and they sort of 'let down their hair,' as it were, with each other. That isn't wrong. It's practically unavoidable. Yet, while we live in such close proximity, each of us does retain a certain amount of privacy, too. Well, that isn't wrong, either.

"The trouble today is that people have been led to believe that if they don't share their inmost secrets and 'let it all hang out,' as you put it, then that is dishonest or psychologically bad. Well, it isn't! And if you want to have secrets from me, you certainly may.

"Now, I want and need your love and affection. But I do not wish to intrude. I'm reaching out to you in love and friendship. And you have a perfect right to reject me. Just as Mabel could have rejected you, or you could have rejected Helen.

"If you wish to reject me, you may. But if you believe our relationship is still profitable to you, then it might be wise to keep our contract in mind. So long as I can help you and you continue to want my help, then so long will we have a relationship that will bring us closer together than we would be as strangers. And in that case, my rules for my property must stand."

I paused and looked at her. She had stopped pacing at

the far side of the room and was staring blankly out a window.

"If I have intruded by asking you about your smoking, then I will ask to be forgiven. I want what is best for you. But I want you to want what is best for you, too. However, *you* are the one who must and will decide."

She was still in profile, fixedly gazing out of the room.

"This is what parents and guardians are for. We've had more experience than those who are younger. That's all. We aren't any smarter; sometimes we aren't even as smart. But we have a more practical scale of value than that of a person who is inexperienced. So, what we hope to do is to save you some of the heartaches that you really don't have to have. That's my position with you.

"Suppose I had said nothing about your smoking. Just ignored it. And then with the passing of time you contracted the habit. Perhaps you'd find it was ruining your health and costing you a great deal of money, and you wished like everything that you'd never started to smoke.

"I think in that case you might look back and say to yourself, 'Well, that stupid old guardian of mine wasn't interested. He just didn't care what I did. He could so easily have given me good advice, but he shrugged it off.' "

Virginia turned and regarded me thoughtfully.

Loy came to the doorway and watched quietly.

"Would you really buy me a pipe if I wanted one?"

"Of course I would. I don't really want to. But here's the way I see the contract we have. I'm going to offer you the best advice and counsel I can. I think I'm obligated to do that. I'm going to provide for your physical wants and see that you get an education. But the most important thing I can do for you and with you is to let you make up your own mind. I have complete trust in you, Gigi. But you are in no position to make up your mind until you have the facts. And I can't provide needed facts if I am unaware of the need. I'll provide all the facts I have at my disposal. *But you must and will decide.* Further, I will abide by your decisions, even if they make me sad. However, I will reserve the right to tell you when you are making me sad.

"Now, if you want to keep things from me, from us, you may do so. I can't and won't compel you. The way I see your end of the contract is this: I think that you are required to respect my rules governing property, because the property involved is mine. I provide it. I think you owe both Loy and me some personal consideration. I think good manners should exist between all of us in this household. We don't want to take advantage of you and I'm sure you don't want to take advantage of us. That means that while I have confidence in you, I will expect you to have a bit of confidence in me, too. And if any of this becomes too irksome, say so, and we can sever the relationship."

Virginia came over and stood in front of me. "Papa, you have been so very kind and good to me. You know I could never do that."

"No, I don't *know* that, Virginia. I do know that you are a profit seeker and will act in terms of your own best interests as you see them. I'm completely sure of that."

"Does that mean that I don't have to mind my own business?"

"No, it doesn't. You will have to mind your own business. But your present business involves Loy and me as contractual partners. And so long as the contract holds, so long will we all be involved. But minding your own business does *not* mean that you have to be secretive. Nor does it mean that you *have* to tell me everything. It does mean that you have to decide for yourself just what you will do and why."

"All right. What are the rules about *your* property that have anything to do with my smoking?"

"Just this. I don't want you shutting Loy and me out of your smoking. If you want a vice, help yourself. But don't feel that you have to rush into your room and sneak a puff. Mind you, I'm not saying you can't smoke in your room. I am only saying that while our partnership continues, I do not want you to shut us out."

"Loy doesn't smoke."

"That's her decision. But if she decided to, I'm sure she wouldn't sneak off to do it."

"I know. I was just thinking. Maybe you'd feel better if we all smoked together."

"It happens that I smoke enough for all three of us. Too much. It's not a good thing to do."

"What if I like to sneak?"

"I'm not trying to forbid that, either, Virginia. Sneak if you find pleasure in it. What I'm trying to make clear is that I am not forcing you to smoke or not to smoke. I am not forcing you to sneak or not to sneak. I want the decision to be all yours. By behaving as you have been, you were making it appear that I had forced you to do certain things in certain ways, which simply is not true. And that's what I had to try to clear up."

"Maybe if we all smoked at the same time, it would be fun. A family that smokes together stays together."

I chuckled. "There may be something in that. A family might be closer if all members shared each other's vices as well as virtues. Not that I'd care to recommend a vice as virtuous."

"Helen smokes pot."

"Does she?"

"I don't. But I do have some of those long, perfumed Turkish cigarettes."

"Do you like them?"

She crinkled her nose. "I hate the taste. Really, they're . . . . " She shuddered.

"Kind of icky?"

She nodded. "They make me cough. I don't like them at all."

"Then why do you use them?"

"Well, I was trying to like them. Helen says that all the 'in' crowd smokes. And drinks. And plays around. And I just knew you'd object, so I was sneaky."

"Of course I object. But I will not forbid you, and there is no point in feeling that you have to sneak. We can have honest differences of view."

"You know, you're not at all the way Helen said you would be. She said you'd raise hell if you caught me. Instead, you want to buy me a pipe. Well, why don't you? Maybe I'd like pipe smoking."

"All right. I'll get you a pipe."

"Can you get one of those hookah pipes that two people can smoke at the same time?"

"I imagine so. Sure you want me to?"

"I really do *not* want to smoke at all."

"All right, Virginia. Then I won't get you a pipe."

"I'm going to throw out those cigarettes."

"Excellent decision."

"I guess I'm just not one of the 'in' people."

"Bosh. Tommyrot. You're as 'in' as anyone. The real 'in' people amount to something in spite of their vices. Getting the vices doesn't make you a part of anything worthwhile."

Suddenly, Virginia was a little girl again. She waltzed to my chair and ran her hand through my hair, rumpling it, as Loy watched.

"Don't you dodge!" And suddenly, before I could do anything about it, I was kissed full on the lips. "There. I've been wanting to do that for a long time!"

She marched from the room with the pride of a Hilary who has just surmounted Everest.

Loy gave me a knowing look, chuckled, and followed Virginia.

Why does a woman always know when a man experiences a secret sense of satisfaction? Probably because a man's secrets aren't as invisible as he thinks.

Chapter 13

THE COST OF SEX

I happened to notice a taxicab drive up to the curb in front of the house. I arrived at the door as the bell rang.

"Taxi," the driver said.

"No one here ordered a cab."

The driver looked at a pad. He repeated our address. "I got the street number right, chief. This here's the place."

"There must be some mistake."

"No mistake. Order came over the radio. Someone phoned."

I shook my head. I heard a shuffling sound and turned. Virginia was staggering down the hall, under the weight of two large suitcases. She ignored me.

"There's a large box in my room, driver," she said. "You'll have to carry it. It's too heavy for me. Don't worry. I'll pay for it."

"Yes, ma'am." He touched his visor and started to come in.

"Whoa, there," I interrupted. "Just what is this all about, Virginia?"

"I'm leaving."

"You're what?"

"I'm leaving."

"Without even saying goodbye or telling us where you're going?"

She was wearing a long coat. Her face communicated stark determination. "It's best that I go, Bob. Please don't ask me anything. Just get out of the way. The quicker I leave, the better for everyone." There was a catch in her voice. I thought I saw a tear.

I was stunned. "Just like that? Virginia! You can't mean it! What has happened?"

"It's . . . well, it's a long story and I've decided it's best not to tell it. So, it's private." She put down the suitcases. "I really am going. You said that if I changed my mind about staying here, it would be all right for me to go. So, I'm going."

"You don't like it here any more?"

"Oh, it's not that." Her voice broke and her face was pinched in sorrow. "If you knew, you'd kick me out anyhow. You and Loy have been wonderful, Bob. I really do appreciate it. But I have to go now. I really do."

I dug in my pocket and handed the driver a bill. "I don't want to hold you up," I said. "You've got to make a living. This'll pay for your trouble. Virginia may be ready to leave, but we have an understanding. Or, at least I was under that impression.

"What I said, Virginia, was that if you decided not to stay, we'd make other arrangements. I distinctly remember saying that *we'd* make the arrangements. That means all of us together."

There was an awkward pause.

"Driver, why don't you go looking for another fare?" I suggested. "If we decide we need a cab, we'll call again."

"Right you are, chief." He went back down the walk.

I turned and surveyed a distraught young lady.

"You had no right to do that, Bob! I called the cab. You are physically stopping me from doing what I want to do."

"No harm done, hon. We can get a cab any time. And I won't prevent you from leaving if you've made up your mind. We've discussed this before. You know I won't stand in your way. But, as your guardian I believe I must know where you are going.

"And you have an obligation, arising out of our close relationship, to at least communicate with me. If I've done some terrible thing so that you don't want to stay with Loy and me any more, I think you owe me a chance to make things right. I'm helpless if I don't know what this is about."

She put her hands over her face and turned toward the wall, convulsed in heartrending sobs.

"Oh, why did you have to interfere? I didn't want you to find out, not ever! Now, it's all ruined. And now you . . . you're making it sound as if *you* did something wrong. As if you could. You or Loy. You're so good. And I'm such a really beastly person."

For a minute or two she sobbed, out of control.

I put my arms around her. She stiffened and tried to push me away. Then suddenly she relented and turning, buried her face against my chest. I let her cry.

Finally, the convulsions stopped. I could feel her body trembling as she struggled for self-control.

"Sweetheart," I said. "I have no idea what this is about. But let's try to make some sense out of it if we can. Loy is out shopping and will be back with the car before long. Either she or I can drive you wherever you're going. Or if you don't want us to, we will call the cab again. But surely we're entitled to some kind of explanation."

"The . . . the truth is, I don't . . . don't really want to go." She was starting to cry again. "You've . . . you and Loy . . . are so darn swell. But this time I've really blown it. You won't want me around . . . any . . . any more at all. I . . . I just thought I'd get out so there . . . there wouldn't be a scene."

Her cheek was running wet where I kissed it. "There, there, hon. If you want to stay, that will be fine. No harm done at all."

She pulled away. "No harm done! Oh, if you only knew. You couldn't say that. I made a terrible mistake, Papa. Oh, it's terrible. I know it now. But . . . well, I did, and that's all there is to it. I've ruined everything. And you'll never speak to me again." She shuddered. "You won't ever even touch me. Ever. Ever." She looked at me with brimming eyes. "You'll never forgive me." Then she started to cry all over again.

"Nothing in the world can be as bad as all this, Virginia. If you had been injured in an accident, or something like that, yes. But you are obviously uninjured in any physical sense."

She tensed and all at once, with strange insight, I knew

her problem although I did not yet know the extent of it.

"Come on. Let's go to my office so we can sit down and talk things over. If you like, we can wait for Loy. But I always find it best to sit down for serious discussion. Somehow, my brain works better when I'm sitting. Funny about that," I said, making conversation as I steered her toward my study. "Maybe a man gets a dizzy brain when it's too far from the floor. I'll have to reflect on that a little longer."

It made no sense, but I had to keep talking. I got her into a chair on the far side of my desk and then sat opposite.

"Should we wait for Loy?"

Virginia shook her head. "No, Bob. I . . . I'm not sure I can tell you. It'll be worse with Loy."

She sat there staring through me. I waited, but she said nothing.

"Can I get you a drink of water? Anything you want so you'll feel better?"

She shook her head. "I . . . I just don't know how to say it."

"Try, sweetheart."

"I . . . I don't know where to begin."

"How about starting at the beginning?"

She heaved a tremulous sigh. Then she focused on my face. "Papa, I thought I was in love with him. Truly." Her eyes fell. "And it should have been so beautiful!"

I nodded. "I gather it wasn't."

She shuddered. She covered her face with her slender hands, and sobs shook her. "It was awful. Oh, I'm so ashamed."

"Before you say another thing, Virginia, I want you to know that I have every confidence in you. I have no idea what you're leading up to. But I'm with you all the way. Okay?"

"It was at Helen's."

"At Helen's house?"

She nodded. "We went there after school. Her folks weren't home. And they have this big rumpus room in the basement. And Harvey and Helen and all the kids were getting smashed. You know. They were drinking and smoking and everyone was having a good time. And they had a stereo and it was belting out some rock. Awful loud. And I was trying to fit in. So, Papa, I had a drink and I guess it went to my head."

"Alcohol isn't really conducive to superior judgment," I said, a knot forming in my stomach.

"Harvey put his arm around me, Papa. And I . . . I was sure he loved me. I was sure he really cared. And, Papa, I felt different than I'd ever felt before. I wanted to be loved. I trusted Harvey. Totally. You just can't know what it was like. I let myself go. I didn't care about anything. I was sure Harvey would take care of me. I felt safe, protected, and wanted." The hands came from her white face and she stared at me. "I acted like a zombie. I just let them make my decisions for me. Helen gave me a pill and I took it. She said it was the only safe way. She said several boys had done it to her, and it was great. And she said I really wouldn't be a woman until it had happened to me. You know. All the way.

"So then Harvey took me upstairs to a bedroom. And we pulled the drapes and we sat on the bed. And Harvey hugged me and kissed me and I wanted him to. And we turned the lights off and he began to undress me. And then he took off his pants. And I knew what he was doing and what was going to happen, although I was embarrassed. At the same time, I didn't want to see him. I just wanted . . . oh, Papa. How can I tell you how I felt? There's just no way."

"My precious girl. You'll never believe it, but I do understand."

"How can you, Papa? How could anyone? My mind wasn't working right. I was feeling a lot of things but I wasn't thinking. And then, just as Harvey was ready to really start, there was a noise outside the bedroom. It was Helen's folks coming upstairs. They had come home.

"We were both scared silly. We got dressed in a hurry and Harvey sneaked out. Then, a bit later, I did, too."

I exhaled audibly. "Was that it, Gigi?"

She nodded mutely.

"I guess you know that I don't approve having anyone else make your decisions for you, Gigi."

Tears started again. "Of course I know that. I wasn't going to tell you. But you always wheedle everything out of me, somehow. So now you know the kind of a person I am. No brains at all."

"Virginia, I hope you will believe me when I say that I understand. I don't admire what you did, but I do understand. The sex drive is very strong in all young people and it's still pretty strong even when you get to be my age. But for goodness sakes, don't go getting the idea that you're dirty and evil. What happened wasn't wise. But it is certainly understandable."

"But, Papa. It wasn't all Harvey's doing. In a way, I led him on. I don't know what I was thinking. Actually, I wasn't thinking. I was being romantic and silly. I guess I just thought we'd kind of blend in mid-air. But the mechanics of it! I don't like that at all. It . . . it's ugly!"

"But you didn't go through with it."

"No, but he still wants to. Only I don't any more. So when he phoned me this morning, I realized that everything was all over. He said he was going to keep after me until we did it together. And he's in school, so he'll see me every day and he'll keep after me. And, Papa, one of these times I'll give in. I know it. I feel it. And that wouldn't be fair to you. You want me to be a thinker. And I'm emotional — all vulnerable inside. I'm weak. I'm a pushover. That's really what I'm really like."

"So you decided that you would leave. Where are you going?"

"To Helen's. I phoned her and they've got an extra room over there.

"And Helen will lend me some money and then I can leave town. I'll go somewhere else. Somewhere I don't have to see him. And I can get a job and pay Helen back and take care of myself. I'm old enough."

"I see."

"Now can we call the cab?" She looked at me, pleading. "It really is best, Papa. Don't you see? If I stay around here, I'll end up doing bad things. And I'll want to. Right now, I don't, but I know what happens to me. Harvey'll get me all excited again and then I'll be just like I was before. I know it."

I reached for one of her hands.

"I don't see why you'd even want to touch me," she said.

"Why, Virginia . . . I love you very much. Nothing has changed at all."

"Nothing has changed!" She was the picture of indignant disbelief. "Everything has changed! I'm a filthy person, Papa. I know it now. I wanted to get laid. And I know I'll want it again. That's the kind of rotten girl I really am."

"Virginia, I haven't talked to you about sexual things. I guess I felt it wasn't up to me. But I was wrong. First, let's straighten out a few things. There is nothing filthy or rotten about sex. It's a perfectly natural and normal thing. If you *didn't* feel that way, I might have cause for alarm. Actually, in view of everything, I think you behaved rather well. Although the arrival of Helen's parents seems to have been a stroke of luck rather than the result of your good judgment, I still have all the confidence in the world in you."

"Papa, you know you don't approve of sex between unmarried people."

"I don't think I ever said that, Virginia. You're right in one sense. I don't approve of irresponsible or promiscuous sexual activities. But one thing I've stressed with you over and over again. No one can rebel intelligently against reality. Sex is a part of reality. And there's nothing wrong with it."

"Well, then, tell me this. Why are so many adults all up tight about it?"

I took a deep breath. "I can't explain why other people act the way they do in this area, Virginia. But let me give you my own reasons. They may not apply to everyone.

"First off, the sex drive is so strong that, as a teacher, I can't compete with it. If I have a class of students and some of the boys and girls are sexually stimulated with each other, my lecture falls on deaf ears. Economic theory simply can't compete. If you and this young fellow were in a class of mine, each of you thinking about the thrill you would have when you got together, you wouldn't hear a word I said. And when you are young, it is important that you learn a great many things besides sex. So I have to face facts. I want your attention. I have to have it in order to explain certain truths.

"Keep in mind that while sex may be important, there are lots of other things in life that are important, too. However, there isn't anything more interesting. So, I think you see where that puts me. I play second fiddle to the biological drive. Every time. So, at least in my classroom I have to ask that the young people refrain from sexual practices at least while I'm teaching them."

For the first time, Virginia's expression lost its tragic appearance. "Oh, Papa. That's funny. Of course you couldn't teach a bunch of people who were wallowing all over each other. Especially if there was rock music going on, too. Oh, my goodness!"

"Good. I'm glad you see that. And there's something more. Remember how, when you and your young man heard footsteps outside the bedroom, you were both frightened? Why? Well, you were involved in something that was very private. You didn't want anyone to find you in that, er . . . situation. Right?"

She nodded. Her lips smiled and then curled down alternatively.

"Actually, adults feel the same way. When adults practice sex, only a very few of them want an audience. Now, I know that some people, probably most of them actors and actresses, may not really mind. But even they aren't all that eager for someone to stand around staring at them when they are engaged in a sexual activity.

"Well, most adults are still embarrassed about sex themselves. They don't want to talk about it. They feel a little ridiculous. The contortions can get to be a bit frantic, as you will one day learn. They like to appear dignified and self-possessed. So, most of them simply shy away from the subject. Or they tell jokes about it because jokes in that area are calculated to remind others of the incongruity and hence the humor of the contradictory situation which sex helps to create for all of us."

"People shouldn't be like that."

"Maybe not, Virginia. But because of the intensity of the drive, the privacy required and all the rest of it, they are often up tight about it and don't like it mentioned. I suppose I'm a bit that way or I probably would have discussed the matter with you myself. You see, sex is a very precious thing. We don't want it profaned. And it's difficult to talk casually about it."

"Papa, I understand that. I really do."

"But probably, Virginia, the biggest reason why adults become tense when they talk to young people about sex, either their own children or other young people, relates to the question of responsibility. Now, there's no particular age at which responsible conduct arrives automatically. Some people mature early and some much later. For example, you and Helen showed a desire to be responsible when she offered you a birth-control pill, and you took it. You wanted the experience but you didn't want the responsibility that pregnancy would have automatically created. One pill wouldn't have protected you.

"Birth-control pills have their limits. To be fully responsible, it might be wise to consult a physician to be sure that the proper birth-control chemical or device is selected. Sometimes there have been serious side effects arising out of dependence on pills.

"And I suspect that enough parents have found themselves with a pregnant daughter on their hands to be pretty worried about all the responsibilities involved. And I can sympathize with them. The young lady has a sexual experience, usually with someone about her own age. The young man is in school, doesn't have a job, and perhaps has a number of years ahead of him as a student before he will be prepared to face life as a productive member of society. If he participates in sex and becomes the father of a child, how can he provide adequately?

"Or, taking the view that the young woman is supposed to provide for herself, what then? Will she be able to finish school, hold down a job, and also take on the absolutely demanding tasks of caring for a small baby?

"As we know, there are costs to everything. While a sexual experience may certainly be profitable to the participants, as we know, Virginia, there is no such thing as a free lunch. TANSTAAFL. And sex does lead to child birth. Not in every case, of course. But thus far, the number of births to occur from something other than a sexual relationship are pretty few in number."

Her eyes were hostile. The levity was poorly timed.

"Look at it through the eyes of an adult, Virginia. You are not yet an adult, although you are certainly growing up fast. Let's suppose that you are through school and on your own. You get a job. At the start, it will be a low-paying job. Everything starts small. Some few may be lucky, but no one can count on luck. So, you have a job and you're just managing to make ends meet. You're paying your way, but no more. And then you become pregnant. What then?

"Who is going to take care of the child when it comes? Who will pay your way when you are forced to stop work? And who will cover the costs of the child, even if you don't lose your job?"

"Papa, the government helps people nowadays if they get into that kind of trouble."

"True enough, Virginia. Sometimes. But the government has nothing of its own. So it has to tax everyone else to provide the money to pay for your child. And that means that you have gone out to have the fun and the thrill of sex and then other people are going to be compelled to cover your costs. I know that's not what you want.

"In fact, you might, as many young girls do, decide not to go through with the pregnancy. What then? Well, you'd have to have an abortion. Or, as you preferred, you have to do something first to prevent pregnancy.

"I think you'll find thousands upon thousands of parents finding that just about as they are beginning to get their feet under them financially, a daughter of theirs becomes pregnant. And because the parents love their daughter, they step in and cover her costs. Or the government does. So, if parents or adults generally ought not to be up tight about sex, I think you can see why many of them are.

"Again, there's nothing wrong with sex when sexual acts are performed by responsible people. But like lots of things that are not wrong in themselves, when people do them in an irresponsible way and others have to step in to cover the costs, that's not a good thing."

"Papa, I'm responsible. You said so yourself. I tried to look after myself."

"True enough, Virginia. And I said you performed fairly well in view of circumstances. But let's take a good look. I'd like to question just how responsible you really were, although you were certainly more so than some.

"First, you had a drink. But why? Was it your first? Did you know how it might affect you? Or were you just doing what others did? I don't think that was very responsible. You are old enough and smart enough to know that alcohol can befuddle the senses and cause people to act irresponsibly. As a matter of fact, I rather imagine that without that drink you probably wouldn't even have gone to the bedroom with the young man.

"Next, you were ashamed of yourself. Was it because of sex, a natural thing, or was it because you had the idea that you were doing a very risky thing that you ought not do?

"Finally, when you faced up to yourself, you decided to leave home without even telling anyone. That was certainly not responsible. We have a beautiful relationship here. Loy and I love you, and respect you."

She started to interrupt, but I continued. "Yes, we still respect you. I do and Loy does. Be sure of that. You don't have a job. You don't have a husband. You probably don't want to marry the young man with whom you got involved. Is it responsible to quit school? Think it through, Virginia. Were you being fully responsible?"

"Papa, I was trying to be fair. I didn't want you to have to pay any more for a bad person like me."

"So you were going to sneak off, leaving me to wonder what had happened? What do you think I would have done? Why, I'd have torn the town apart trying to find you. I could have quit work, spent days and weeks hunting for you. The costs to me would have been tremendous. I might have thought you'd been kidnapped. I could have imagined all kinds of things happening to you. Do you think I would just have shrugged and let it pass?"

"Well, you've said that you trusted me. Why couldn't you have just accepted that I was all right and was just minding my own business?"

"In the kind of world we have, Virginia? Come, you know the answer to that. How many young girls vanish every year never to be heard from again? Some are killed or kidnapped. Some are sold into enforced prostitution . . . with no escape. Some get involved romantically with some green and callow youth, move away, and then the lad deserts the girl. And she's so ashamed of her bad judgment that she tries to make her way alone.

"Hon, I hope this whole event turns into a valuable lesson. I think you are a very wonderful person. You're as smart as they come. And you're fully normal in all ways. Including sex. So, you've got a good future ahead of you if you act responsibly.

"You might think of it this way. The party who is responsible is ready, willing, and *able* to cover *all* costs arising from his actions.

"I know that you're ready and willing. But are you really *able?* At thirteen? Gosh, sweetheart, I'm not any more than just able myself, and I've had three times your experience."

Her eyes were downcast. "Go ahead. Ball me out. I have it coming."

"Okay, if it pleases you. Consider yourself balled out. I think I've said all that needs saying."

We sat at the desk for a moment.

"It's like economics, isn't it, Papa?"

"In what way?"

"Responsibility. TANSTAAFL. All that. You said a responsible person is one who is ready, willing, and able to pay all the costs arising from his actions."

"Right."

"I'm not, am I?"

"No, my dear. You're not. I know that the years seem long and time seems to drag and there are so many things you want to do and to experience. You probably feel that life is rushing past you. But it isn't. Not at all. The day will come when you will be able to be fully responsible. That's what I believe, and it's toward that end that I'm working. Believe me, I want it. I want your maturity. And you'll have it when you think through to the result that *might* arise out of your actions, and then prepare yourself in advance to meet all the costs."

"I'm sorry, Papa. I've given you a bad time."

I nodded. "Yes, you have. But it's over now. Everything is fine."

"You don't think I'm completely impossible?"

"Of course not. And I must say I think the young man showed excellent taste in choosing you as his bed partner. But I'm awfully glad it got no further than it did. There's plenty of time for that, sweetheart. Later. Quite a few years from now. Now is the time for you to buckle down and get a lot more learning into that pretty head of yours."

"All right, Papa." She looked up and smiled. "I'm going to break off with Helen. That way I can create a little gap between Harvey and me."

"Harvey? I wondered about that, but I wasn't going to ask."

"Yes, it's Harvey. I'll tell you something else. It shows what a devious, deceitful creature I can be. The reason I wanted to take the cab over to Helen's was so I could be near Harvey again. Isn't that awful? I don't love him. But I was thinking that maybe . . . well, maybe it just might work out and we could do it and then I'd go away and no one would know where I was."

"Thank you for telling me." I looked at her closely. What else was hidden behind that smooth forehead, the soft, almost baby cheeks, the look of innocence? Virginia had grown to emotional maturity. How fortunate I was that such total communication between us was still possible.

"Harvey's the real reason, Papa. He's a year younger than Helen, but he's awfully big for his age."

I smiled. "You might keep this in mind, my dear. Remember what we've said about value. I know I often seem like an old fuddy-duddy to you, but the fact remains that I know how value works. We value and appreciate those things that are in scarce supply. If you make yourself readily available to Harvey or to anyone else, their estimation of you will go down. I'm not suggesting that you become aloof or distant. Be yourself. In my younger days, a girl who was instantly willing we called a 'pushover.' And she got to be a joke among the fellows. Such a girl was too easy. And we didn't value her friendship after a bit. I'm going to suggest that you place a high value on yourself. You're worth it. And when you find the young man you really love, if you do, then get him to show that he's worthy of you in every way before you decide to make it easy for him. Does that sound like good advice?"

"Papa, you make me realize just how lucky I am. Our relationship is really pretty great. It's got more in it than I thought."

"I'm glad you feel that way."

"Do you still like me?"

"Very much. You're my girl. I don't know if I can pretend that you're my *little* girl any more. But you are a very, very special girl to me and you always will be."

Chapter 14

MONEY AND PRICES

The easy chair in front of the fireplace was large and comfortable. I puffed my pipe in solid content, reflecting on the excellent meal Loy had served and idly watching Virginia as she bent over a book, her hair dangling over her face, screening everything from her mind except the words on the page. At least I presumed as much.

She no longer confided in me totally. I couldn't expect that. No one is ever able to fully communicate his innermost reality. I thought of the several years she had been our guest and noted how she had matured. There had been problems. But the lovely young lady sitting on the far side of the room was surely ample reward for the few difficulties.

It would be nearly two years before she could enter college. But she had evidently acquired a thirst for knowledge and a willingness to concentrate in its pursuit.

Of course, I was prejudiced. But it seemed to me that she was as advanced as many college freshmen I had seen or even up to the level of second-year students on major campuses.

She was engrossed in her book and I didn't interrupt. I may have dozed. The sound of Virginia's voice stirred my idling mind.

"I really don't know whether to believe this stuff or not, Papa."

"What stuff, hon?"

"The stuff I've been reading."

I looked at her quizzically and she got the message.

"Sorry. Of course you don't know what I'm reading, do you. It's American history. It seems to me to be full of contradiction."

"I suspect it is. History is particularly difficult to write with any degree of detachment. Whoever the historian is, he is bound to see things through his own eyes and to report those items he believes to be important."

"Papa, I know. And I appreciate that. It's just that at school the teachers seem to want you to accept everything you read as authoritative. If you do, you get high marks. If you don't, they think you're dumb."

"What's troubling you, hon?"

"This history book makes it appear that the American people — he uses a general collective term to imply the entire European population in America — all wanted to set up a republic. But earlier in the book he explained that most of the people in the new world had had no education. Most of them could neither read nor write. And then he also says that John Adams figured that at the time of the American revolution only about a third of the American people favored breaking off from England. So, what am I to believe?

"If the American people in general were uneducated, they wouldn't have known a republic from any other form of government. If John Adams is right, then only a minority favored the war with England. And if either of these things is true, then the historian ought not to make it appear that the American people, as a single collective, agreed on anything."

My appreciation for her astute observation must have been carried by my voice. "Very good, Virginia. You are thinking. That is the most important part of going to school. Learning to think and to think critically."

"But what am I to believe?"

"Put yourself in the position of the historian, my dear. In one sense, you may even have an advantage over him, however erudite he may be. You know something about human nature. You understand a few of the basic economic principles. For instance, the historian may be correct on each point, even though the points appear to conflict. The reason is that people change their minds. People aren't consistent, as you know. Think how the opinions of the colonists must have vacillated. Opinions are like values. They shift around.

"And you might keep in mind that all knowledge is contextual. In one context, it might be a good thing to recall that few of the American settlers had had formal schooling. Good point. In another context, it might be wise to keep John Adams' ideas in mind concerning the numbers of persons who favored a break with England. In still another context, it might be entirely satisfactory to refer to the American people in general since they would surely have had some things in common however they may have differed in a particular case. I think you are using your head. If I were your history teacher, I would be proud of you."

Virginia's face was sunshine itself. "He is, Papa. I'm sure he likes me. He gives me good grades."

"And it's not from just parroting back what he says, either. Right?"

She nodded. "You really do have to be broad-minded, don't you, Papa? You have to keep a lot of different things in your mind all the time."

"Splendid. You are thinking like a praxeologist. When you get the basics fully in mind, then you begin to see the ramifications. You are doing a splendid job."

She shut the book. "Well, I've covered the assignment, anyhow. I wish you were my teacher, Papa. You make everything so interesting."

"I've been thinking, Gigi . . . Virginia. One of the things I've neglected talking to you about is the subject of money and banking. Or the two subjects of money and banking. If you have your studies conquered for the evening, perhaps we could consider the question of money."

"You've already explained it, Papa."

"I have?"

"Sure. Money is what we use to buy things with."

"That's a good beginning. But what is it?"

"Well, I just said. It's what we use to buy things with."

"All right. We call it a medium of exchange. Why do we call it a 'medium'?"

"Oh, I don't know. Maybe because there are several kinds of money?"

"Not necessarily. Although I wouldn't rule that out. We call it a medium because it is in the middle. All full exchanges, Virginia, are really barter. We exchange something for something else. But to make barter easy, we usually don't trade directly. We trade indirectly. That is, we take the goods or services we have and we exchange them for money. Then, with the money we purchase other goods and services. When the exchange is complete, we've traded into money and out again. So, money is the medium, the thing in the middle."

"Why go to all that bother?"

"Because it's the easiest way. For instance, if you were raising corn for a living and we didn't use money, then when you wanted something other than corn, you'd have to use your surplus of corn to get whatever you wanted. Suppose you wanted to buy a car. Before you could, you'd have to find someone with a car willing to exchange the car for several tons of corn. That might be hard to do. How many people selling cars are really looking for tons and tons of corn in exchange?"

"I never looked at it that way. But I see it. Golly."

"It's not only true about corn and cars, it's true about everything. The economic system we have is one that functions best when we practice what is called a division of labor. I work at my job. Others work at theirs. Instead of making direct exchanges, we almost always trade into money. That is, we are paid for our work in money. And then, when we have the money, we can buy whatever else we want rather than practicing direct barter. It's much the better way."

Virginia showed excitement. "I remember now. My math teacher said something like that one day, only I didn't understand what he meant. But I do now. It would be pretty silly trying to trade houses for sandwiches or an automobile for a dress. You have to have money!"

"Right. Money is very important. Now, what is money?"

She frowned. "You've just said. It's a medium of exchange."

"I want to bring out another point. Money, Virginia, is an abstract term. There is no such *thing* as money. Many different things can be used as money, but there is no *one* thing that is automatically money. In fact, since we first began to improve on direct barter, thousands and thousands of years ago, many different things have been used and are used as money. We've used various grains and root crops. We've had cattle, pigs, sheep, and goats. Cocoanuts. Hemp. Salt. Sugar — a host of food items. But in addition, we've used pins, lumber, cloth, cigarettes, soap, chocolate bars. One of the most important and best items we've ever come across for use is gold. Silver isn't far behind."

She shook her head. "That's not what they tell me in school, Papa. We don't need gold. They say that money is really faith; faith in the government. And if people had enough faith, we'd never have any money problems."

"Curiously, there's something to that, hon. The belief people have in their government is very close to a religious conviction. In consequence, when a government obtains the confidence of its people, it can use almost anything as money and the people will accept it. Many primitive tribal chiefs got their subjects to use cowrie shells for money. The Yapese even today use huge boulders as money. The smallest weigh about two tons.

"In the United States today, what do most of us use for money?"

"Oh, I know the answer to that. Paper. We have dollar bills. And that's what we use as money. Paper."

"Yes, we certainly do have paper currency. But it isn't the basic item, although many people think it is. Now listen carefully, for here's where the banks come in. The major item we use as money in this country is no more than a bookkeeping entry in a bank."

Virginia wrinkled her nose. "I don't understand that, Papa. That sounds crazy."

I nodded. "Money isn't easy to understand. But if you get the basics right, you'll understand it well enough, although I must say this is the area where most economists have their major differences.

"Let's follow a transaction step by step. Let me suppose that you have a job and at the end of a week you get a pay check. What is a check?"

"Oh, that's something the company writes. Or a person.

Private people write checks, too."

"Of course they do. We use checks as money. I write checks myself when I want to pay bills. But let's take it one step at a time. You get paid by check. Chances are good that you'll take it to a bank and open a bank account. It's a great convenience. So you turn the check over to the bank and they give you a pass book with an entry on the first page indicating that you have deposited the amount of your check in their bank. Let's suppose your check was $100. Your pass book would indicate that you had a hundred dollars in the bank."

"Well, what's wrong with that? That's what I'd have, all right. A hundred dollars." Her eyes were shining at the prospect of so much money.

"But wait, Virginia. Where is the currency? You didn't put $100 worth of currency in the bank, all you put there was a check. Where's the currency?"

She laughed. "Thought you could fool me about that, didn't you? Well, you can't. My math teacher explained that. The company that I'm working for has the currency in their account and so they just take $100 in currency out of the company's account and put it in mine."

"But wait, hon. That's too fast. The chances are good that the company for which you work doesn't have any currency in its account, either. They get paid by checks. Most of their customers write checks to pay their bills and those checks are deposited in the company account. All the company has in its account, for the most part, is a bookkeeping entry, or a series of them."

She looked at me in astonishment. "Oh, no, Papa. They'd have to have money there or the check wouldn't be any good."

"Think again, Virginia. You didn't put any money in your account when you deposited the check, but if you write a check the bank will make good on it. And that's what happens all the time. The medium of exchange we use, oh, as much as ninety per cent of the time, is nothing but bookkeeping entries placed in various accounts and then shifted around on the basis of checks written by the people who have the accounts. That's all there is to it."

"But there's got to be money behind it somewhere."

"No, there doesn't, hon. This is where the faith comes in. Faith is a derivative of what we call credit. And credit is a promise to make good. If the promise is kept, everything is fine.

"Go back to our step-by-step process. You get paid by check and a bookkeeping entry is made. You write a check against that figure. The bank debits your account and credits the account of the party who receives the check. If you establish good credit and use checks to pay your bills, you could, in fact, pay everything by check, get paid by check, and never at any time have any currency or other form of money in your hands. Now, most of us don't go to that extreme. We usually keep a few dollars in currency and small change around for incidentals, for impulse spending. But by far and away the prevalent form of money we use in this country is that kind of money — bookkeeping entries. In short, we use credit as money. And that's faith. Faith in the company for which you work and faith in you by those who trust that your check will be good when you write it and they accept it. Billions of dollars change hands every day in this fashion without a single piece of currency in evidence."

"Are you sure about that, Papa?"

"Yes, hon, I'm quite sure."

She nodded. "Then I see what they meant at school. This is why we don't need gold. All we need is faith and then the bookkeeping entries will be fine."

"It seems like that, doesn't it? But that isn't really true. You have to go deeper than that. Let's take the next step. What will your money buy?"

"Anything I want in the store. That is, if I have enough to pay for it."

"True enough. But what is a dollar worth?"

Again she laughed. "Unless there's some trick to your question, a dollar is worth one hundred pennies or two fifty-cent pieces or four quarters or ten dimes or twenty nickels. I had that in school."

"That doesn't really answer my question, hon, although it seems to. You've merely stated different ways of adding up to a dollar. But however you add it up, what will the dollar buy?"

"A dollar's worth of something?"

"True. But how much of that something is a dollar's worth?"

"Golly. I don't know."

"Precisely. You don't know. No one does. Like everything else, money hasn't any fixed or objective value. A dollar is worth exactly what you can buy with it at the time you spend it. If prices rise, you buy less with your dollars. If prices fall, you buy more. Now, if you examine that, it tells us a great deal about money. Remember the principle concerning value. We tend to value things in terms of their relative scarcity. Thus, if more and more money is provided, either through the printing of paper or through the granting of more and more credit, more and more paper or credit dollars will be in circulation. And as more and more dollars are provided, each dollar will buy less. This means that an increase in the amount of paper or credit money will cause each unit of money to purchase less. In short, prices go up."

Virginia's mouth was open. She was staring at me in growing comprehension. "Oh, my. Is that why prices keep going up all the time? I thought it was because of everyone seeking profits, being greedy."

"Partly, Virginia. There are a number of causes which can engender a price rise. For instance, if there is an established demand for a given good or service and that good or service falls into scarce supply, prices will rise. Or, if a demand increases in any area, that, too, can cause prices to rise in that area.

"When prices are administered by government decree, that usually forces prices upward. Any tax simply increases the cost of whatever is being sold and that puts prices up. Union demands, when approved, frequently cause a rise in prices. An extensive reliance upon credit buying causes prices to rise. The use of poor money causes prices to rise. There are just lots and lots of things that can push prices up. But one of the most important is the increase in the supply of whatever we are using for money: credit, paper, gold, silver — it doesn't matter. When our media-in-exchange enlarges in its total supply, prices tend to rise. So there is no fixed amount of anything that is a 'dollar's worth.' A dollar is worth what you can get for it when you spend it."

"Papa, I don't understand all of that."

"Let me say it more slowly. A step at a time. Okay? If more people want a given item or decide to buy more of that item, there will be more dollars appearing to purchase that item than were available before for that item. The result is that the total units of the good will be smaller than the total number of dollars bid by buyers for that item. Let's take an example: soy beans. Let's suppose that in a given year a thousand tons of soy beans are grown. And let's assume that customers have been buying just about that amount every year. Then someone discovers a new use for soy beans. Immediately, more people want to buy. Storekeepers find that the demand for soy beans has grown. So they turn to the producers of soy beans to replenish their supplies. But the people who produce the beans haven't grown enough of them. To slow down demand until the new supply shows up, retailers begin to charge more. They don't like to run out. When they run out of something, they feel a little stupid."

"Papa, that isn't really it, is it? Businessmen raise prices so they can make more money. Everyone knows that. And you said yourself that everyone is after all he can get. We all want to make profits."

"Hon, this is probably the one place more than any other where people are confused about how a market works. It almost seems as though people have to get into business themselves, to experience this first-hand, before they comprehend it.

"But let's see if I can make it clear. First of all, the farmer finds out that he didn't grow enough soy beans. How does he find it out? The people who need more beans ask him to supply them and he doesn't have them. So he knows he has to raise more as soon as possible.

"Now, the average person thinks that planting more beans is a 'cost free' operation. He forgets TANSTAAFL. For the farmer to plant more beans, he probably has to go to the bank to borrow money so he can buy more seed, prepare more land, and do all the other costly things that have to be done in order to get the beans. You see, the farmer doesn't have that kind of money. He's been operating at a different level. Now he has to boost production. That costs money.

"But ultimately the farmer has nowhere to get the money, really, except from his customers. Of course he can borrow from the bank temporarily, but that has to be repaid, plus interest. In the end, the customer must pay. So the first thing the farmer does is to notify his customers that as of such and such a date in the future he will have a larger supply of soy beans available. But the price will be higher. Why? Because the farmer has to cover the additional costs to which he has been put in order to increase production. And he must meet that at once.

"What else happens? The wholesaler who buys from the farmer is notified of the new higher price. But he doesn't have the money in his pocket to pay that higher price. Let's suppose that he has a few pounds of soy beans left. He will immediately raise the price to the retailer, not to 'make more money' as everyone thinks, but to offset the increased costs to himself when he buys soy beans in the future.

"The whole process continues to repeat. The grocer has some few bags of soy beans left on his shelf. Now the wholesaler notifies him that next year the new crop will be sold at a higher figure. Where will the grocer get the money? All his money, too, comes from his customers. So he puts the price up at once in order to get the money together so that next year he can stay in business and still retail soy beans. Not a single one of these people is trying to take advantage of customers. Each is trying to stay in business — sometimes desperately trying. And often, even though it appears that they are making huge profits, they don't even begin to get the money together that is necessary for them to stay in business at the same level as before."

"Papa, I still don't get it."

"Let's talk about peanut butter, hon. I know you like that. Here is a grocer who buys peanut butter in pound jars or cans. Let's suppose he keeps one hundred jars in stock and that the cost to him is fifty cents a jar. That means he has $50 tied up in peanut butter. Now his overhead, let us suppose, amounts to another fifteen cents per jar, including wages, lights, heat, telephone, rent, insurance, reserves, and so on. So he's been selling his fifty-cent peanut butter at sixty-five cents. He makes about a penny a jar, plus covering his other overhead costs.

"Now the wholesaler says to him, 'Mr. Grocer, when you want to buy peanut butter next month, the price to you is going to be sixty cents instead of fifty.' The grocer does some quick figuring. He is going to have to invest $60 in peanut butter instead of $50 if he is to remain in business as before. Now, where will he get that extra $10? He doesn't have it. He doesn't want to borrow, for that, too, adds to his costs. Interest is a very expensive addition to all the other costs he must pay.

"So he immediately raises the price on all the peanut butter he has in stock. He stamps it seventy-five cents instead of sixty-five cents. And his customers become furious. They say, 'Look at the rip-off artist! He's already paid for this peanut butter and now he's taking advantage of us. He's just raking in ten cents more per jar and putting it in his own pocket.

"But that isn't what the grocer is doing at all. He's just trying to stay even with the board. The money to buy future supplies has to come from his customers and he has to get that money out of his existing stock before he can buy more stock. That's why he raises his price.

"Do you see that, hon?"

"Oh, my golly. Oh. Oh, my. Yes, I do, Papa. I never thought of it that way."

"The reason prices go up isn't because businessmen *want* to charge more. Actually, as I showed you with our Mr. Newton, every businessman from first to last *must* offer a saving and a benefit to his customers. There are no exceptions at all. And if he wants to stay in business, he must take in enough money so he can produce more, or wholesale more, or retail more. He doesn't want his customers to think he's going out of business. For then they would stop buying from him and turn to a competitor."

"So he charges more because he *doesn't* want to make profits? That's what it sounds like, Papa."

"No, he charges more because he believes it is better for him to stay in business and that way he'll make more over the long pull. Of course, when you get a cost-push rise in prices, some figure it isn't worthwhile any more and they go out of business. They may sell cheaper because they only have to get their money out of it. They're not looking ahead except to their retirement. But to the man who wants to stay in operation, he must get the money from his customers *now* to pay for what he buys in the future."

"Oh, I see that. If he doesn't get the extra now, then he won't be able to buy from the wholesaler the things his customers want more of. The grocer doesn't want to say, 'We don't carry soy beans.' That might discourage his customers from coming back." She clapped her hands. "I've gone shopping with Loy and it happens quite a lot. The grocer always tells Loy that he'll have what she wants a little later, he never says that he's going to run out. He wants to stay in business."

"Of course. Now, that illustrates what happens when there's an increased demand for an established product. Let's take a look from a different angle. Take gasoline. Because of a series of factors relating to international politics, war, ecological efforts to preserve the environment, and increased costs in many areas, plus a number of laws that simply tie everything up in a knot, we began to experience a real shortage of gasoline. Not enough was being produced. To stretch out supplies, oil companies began raising prices. By doing so, assuming they were free to do so, they could go out and try to bring in new fields so they could produce more and sell more."

"Papa, the kids say that the gasoline shortage isn't real. That rich and greedy oil companies deliberately kept the gasoline off the market so they could raise the price."

"I know. And there certainly was a bit of maneuvering here by various companies, each one jockeying for a favorable position. But the truth is, hon, that no company gets rich unless it sells. And I don't care how rich the company seems to be, it can go broke in short order if it doesn't sell. There are enough oil companies so that they are very competitive. Each one wants to sell more than the others so each can make more. And they don't make any money without selling. I remember hearing common gossip that General Motors, for instance, was so rich and powerful that nothing could happen to hurt it. And then people stopped buying cars. General Motors was in real financial trouble in ninety days! You have to sell if you're in business. GM laid off thousands of workers. It just doesn't matter how rich you are. Many of the most potent companies we've ever had in the country ended by going bankrupt. It doesn't take long. In fact, the bigger you are, the quicker you can lose huge sums of money. You have to sell if you're in business."

"I never looked at it that way."

"Virginia, there's nothing magic about anything. Keep the rules of reality in mind. Business is like a living entity. Just as you and I have to eat every day, so a businessman has to sell all the time. Oh, we might survive a few days without food and a businessman could survive a short time without sales. But only a short time. And then he'd be right up against reality. He'd be forced to quit. Or he'd have to make sales. One or the other."

"Is that always true?"

"Just as true as that you and I have to eat to live.

"Now, let's take a look at administered prices. When government begins to set prices for various goods and services, the law of supply and demand no longer functions well. So businessmen are faced with the necessity of rushing to Washington to plead with government to let them raise their prices. While there are exceptions here, almost all government interventions in the price schedule push prices upward. For one thing, keeping the government in that position requires swarms of government workers. They have to be paid. And that means that the more we run to government for help, the larger the tax bill grows. And then, as taxes are collected, the cost of everything else goes up, for a tax is a cost added to whatever we buy. We surely know that. And again, there is no magic. Given a free market, one in which the government does not intervene, prices tend to stay down. Customers can be ruthless and will demand excellent goods and fine services or they'll take away their patronage. If they do, the firm goes broke. But the government tries to be kind-hearted. So if a businessman is in trouble because customers aren't buying enough, the government tries to help the businessman so he won't go broke.

"Union demands do the same thing, if the demands are granted. The wages paid by a businessman are a major cost. If that cost gets bigger, he passes it on to his customers. You've probably heard that the businessman ought to cut down on his profits. But actually, his profits are usually quite marginal. What really happens is that the businessman never pays any cost or any tax. He just passes those things along and his customers foot the bill. Calling for taxes on the businessmen is about as silly as anything can be. They don't really pay any taxes at all. Actually, the businessman doesn't even provide his own tax money that he pays on his personal income. His salary or wage and all the taxes paid on it must come from his customers. In all economic thinking, Virginia, you have to start from zero and then figure all the factors. But I think you see that.

"I believe I said that extensive reliance upon credit buying also causes a price rise. I was thinking primarily of budget buying. Budget buying is a kind of credit. The customer wants a new refrigerator, let us suppose. He goes to the store and finds that for $400 he could buy a new model. But he doesn't have $400 in cash. However, if he pays $50 down and $25 a month for two years, he can have a refrigerator delivered at once. That fits into his budget and he buys. But he is paying $650 for a $400 refrigerator. After awhile, people stop worrying about what the total price is. They are only concerned in finding out if the payments fit into their budget. And that tends to push up prices tremendously.

"Finally, Gigi, when poor money or bad money is in circulation, we get the same result."

"What do you mean by 'bad money'?"

"Virginia, have you ever had a counterfeit coin, or a foreign coin that at first glance looks like one of ours? Most of us have. And what do most of us do if that happens? Why, we pass it along as quick as we can. And we really couldn't mind spending a few extra counterfeit coins for something because we suspect the coins of being counterfeit and think ourselves lucky if we can buy anything at all.

"Often, people are very canny, very shrewd about money, without understanding why they act the way they do. When people make lots of money without much effort;

or when they have it handed to them with no effort; or when credit is easy; or when the money they have is backed by nothing at all except promises and faith, people begin to have an uneasy sense that the money isn't worth much. And of course it usually isn't, for the supplies of that kind of money can be increased endlessly and instantly. When that happens, they begin to treat whatever money they have as though it is counterfeit. They are willing to spend more of it than before because they aren't really sure the money will buy anything. And this helps to put prices up. The circulation of 'bad money' then is one of the factors that helps to increase costs. The money is buying less and less with each passing day. So they don't want to hang onto it. They don't trust it. It will buy less tomorrow than it does today. So they don't mind exchanging their money for goods at a little higher price. Of course, the goods will ultimately wear out. Everything does. Nothing is permanent. But they think that the things they buy will retain a value *longer* than the money because the money isn't really very good. So they exchange in favor of their own best interests, as always. And they spend freely, being willing to pay more just to get something for their money *now,* rather than getting something less for their money *later.*"

"Oh, my." Virginia shook her head. "Don't say anything for a minute, please. I want to think about all that. Oh, my."

"It's worth thinking about, hon."

"Golly, no wonder everything costs so much."

"Right."

She nodded slowly. After a few moments, she said, "I think I understand it."

"Very good. And that brings me back to gold. If what we use as money is mostly credit money—checks, or currencies made of paper—and if the government has complete control of that credit or currency, as ours does, the government can increase the amount of currency or credit any time it cares to do so. And people constantly clamor for more money. So politicians, in order to be popular and to do good things, constantly try to do what the people ask them to. So the government keeps on increasing the supply of currency and credit, and prices keep going up."

She nodded mutely.

"Now, hon, if the currency or credit were tied to something like gold or silver; something that is scarce because nature has not provided very much of it; something that lasts; something that people like and trust; then the government's ability to increase the amount of currency or credit would be limited. They couldn't increase the supplies of currency or credit beyond the *reality* of the existing supply of gold or silver."

"But then there wouldn't be very much money around."

"There certainly wouldn't be as much around as there is now."

"But, Papa, that could be very bad."

"Wait a minute, hon. You're forgetting something. Money of whatever kind has no real or fixed value. Money is worth what you can get for it at the time you spend it. For example, if you earned $100 a week and with that $100 you could buy X, Y, and A, you'd be able to live at that level. But if your wages were cut to $75 and with the $75 you could buy X, Y, Z, and Q, you'd be better off with the smaller amount of money. Wouldn't you?"

"Say that again."

I repeated the statement. "Now, have in mind that the government wants to be kind. People in government positions become popular because they win a reputation for being kind and generous. So, why doesn't the government simply print a million dollars for everyone in the country and mail it to them tomorrow? Everyone in the country would become a millionaire overnight."

She laughed. "That would be wonderful. Oh, Papa, do you think that could happen if we elected the right people? That's what Henry wanted to do."

"Well, let's think about it. What would you do if you were through school and suddenly got your hands on a million dollars? Would you go out to get a job?"

"Certainly not. I'd travel. Oh, I'd love to travel all around the world. And with a million dollars, I could easily do that."

"How would you do it, Virginia? When you went to the airport, it would be closed. Everyone at the airport, from the porters to the pilots, would have quit so they could spend their lives in leisure. They wouldn't want to work, either. So, who would fly you? Or drive your train? Or pump gas for you at a filling station? Or bring the gas to the station when it ran out?"

"Why would they quit?"

"Why did you decide not to get a job?"

"Would everyone quit?"

"Probably not quite everyone. There would always be a few people who wanted to work for nothing because they like their work that much. But they wouldn't want your money. They have all the money they would ever want so they wouldn't want any more. You see, Gigi, people accept money only because they believe they can get rid of it advantageously. That's what makes money good. Other people wanting it. You can't wear the money or eat it or live in it. It is only good at the time you get rid of it. And you can only get rid of it by giving it to people who don't have enough of it. If everyone had enough of it, then no one would take any more. If no one would be willing to work to get more, then the money would be useless."

"Papa, it's pretty complicated."

"It is at that. But you must understand it. Again, money is a medium of exchange. A transfer agent. That's all it is. It isn't wealth. If you lived on a desert island and had a billion dollars but there was nothing on the island for you to buy, the money would be worthless. In fact, in that situation, even if you had a billion dollars, you'd be terribly poor."

"I'm beginning to see that."

"Fine. So money is important and valuable because it is in scarce supply. And it is and always will be unevenly divided. That's the reality of money. A country is rich because it has goods and services, not because it has money. Unfortunately, most people think in terms of money. And you can fool yourself very badly that way. You get to think that the more money you have, the richer you are. Actually, money is only useful if it has purchasing power. And purchasing power is related directly to what you can buy with it. Money without purchasing power is just trash."

"That's why gold is important, huh?"

"Let's be sure I say this correctly. There's nothing magic about gold, either. Gold is just a metal. Most people think it's a beautiful metal, but that's a subjective point of view. It's just a metal. The important thing about it is two-fold. First, it's scarce. It's hard to produce and it's hard, very hard, to increase the total supply. So if what we use as money is tied to it in some way, it's very hard to increase the total supply of money. And that would be good. For then the money that we have would buy more and more. And that's what's really important. If we had a free market in money, people might not be so eager to get a wage increase. They wouldn't have to. Because if money were tied to gold, it would be easier to increase the total supply of goods and services than to increase the supply of money. And as goods and services became more plentiful against a relatively stable supply of money, your money would buy more. So you'd be getting a *real* wage increase without even asking for it. Your money would buy more and more. Because prices would begin to decline year by year and even day by day."

"It's just the opposite of the way things are now."

"Right. But I said there were two major advantages to using gold — the first being its natural scarcity. The second is really peculiar, but it's true all the same. Money is important, as I've just stated, because *other people* want it. The first requirement of a truly useful money is its acceptability. The more people are willing to accept it, the more useful that substance or thing is, as money. Now, for some strange reason that I cannot explain, people want gold. They trust it. In fact, they even say they 'love' it. Why they feel that way isn't clear. As I said, there's nothing magic about it. It's just a metal. Now, the job of the market is to provide what people want. And over thousands and thousands of years of experience, we have learned that people love and want gold. It is the most universally accepted thing we've ever used as money.

"As long as people want it, why not let them have it? Curiously, they rarely want to spend the gold. They get it and they keep it. So, gold by itself as the only money probably wouldn't do. But if we used paper or credit money, backed by gold, then if people lost their faith in a businessman or in the government, as they are bound to do from time to time, they could always beat a retreat and exchange their credit or their currency for gold. And that would make them happy. It would satisfy them. And I, for one, want to see people satisfied."

"But it does come back to faith, doesn't it?"

"In a sense, yes. But faith, Virginia, unless it is a hollow, unjustified faith, has to be based on reality. If you want to be trusted, you have to demonstrate that you are trustworthy. And most businessmen do this. And most government people want to be trusted, too. Sometimes people deserve to be trusted and sometimes they don't. But there's no fooling around with gold. It is! And it is what it is! So, if at any time your currency or your credit was convertible into gold, then your money would be more trustworthy. You'd not only have the justifiable trust in people part of the time but, in addition, you'd have something real and sure behind what you were using as money."

I stopped talking and watched the changing expressions on Virginia's face.

"Papa, I'm going to have to think about that quite a while. If I forget something, can I ask you about it later?"

"Of course, my dear."

"There's one thing I've been meaning to ask."

"Very well."

"It's about my allowance."

I chuckled. "Now, that's what I get for turning your attention to the subject of money."

"But Papa, it's true. My allowance isn't enough any more. Everything costs so much! I really need a raise."

"Are you sure? My salary is the same as it was and I have to make do with what I have."

"But you have a lot more than I do, Papa."

"My expenses are slightly more, too, hon. Tell you what. I know you don't like math, but why don't you put down on a slip of paper where your present allowance goes? Keep track of it for this next week, jotting down where you spend your money. Then let me look at that account. If you can justify an increase in your allowance, I'll provide it and buy a cheaper brand of tobacco. Okay?"

"Do I have to?"

"You do want the raise?"

"Oh, all right. I just knew that arithmetic would come into it sooner or later."

"Arithmetic is part of life, hon. But give me some credit. I haven't relied on mathematics or arithmetic to teach you quite a bit about economic matters."

"All right, Papa. I'll give you credit if you give me more cash!" She laughed merrily and came over to my chair.

"Papa, I appreciate you very much. I wonder if you know that." Suddenly, she was in my lap, her arms around my neck. "You are a dear, adorable person, Papa. You are my very most best friend." She kissed my cheek, ran her hand through my hair, and then was off in a swirl of skirt and dancing legs on her way to her room.

Chapter 15

POLITICS

"Virginia!"

"Yes, Papa." Her voice came from her room.

"If you're not too busy, please come to the study."

In a moment, she appeared. A beaded Indian headband kept her dark hair in place. She wore a beige suit, soft and wooly, with her well-shaped legs twinkling below the mini-skirt. Her face was wreathed in smiles.

"Hello, Papa. Thanks for calling me. I was beginning to get bored. I've decided to write a novel but my heroine is getting a little stuffy. Of course, I like her. But she's an awful lot like me. And that can be pretty boring."

"I want to talk to you about something that is very serious."

She looked at my face and her smile faded. "What is it, Papa? Is something wrong?"

"Not really, hon. Not in the way your question points. There's no family crisis, so far as I know. The status is quo."

She sighed.

I moved a chair close to mine so she could sit facing me without the desk between us.

"I'm glad there's no big hang-up," she said. "You looked so serious. I thought maybe I'd done something wrong again."

"What do you mean, 'wrong again'? Does it seem to you that I'm always correcting you?"

"I suppose it does." She sat, knees together, feet on the floor. I remembered when her legs were so short they dangled. "Of course, if I stop to think about it, I know better. But I guess that's the way it is with people when they get older, isn't it? They don't mean to be that way, but they kind of pick, pick, pick."

I started to protest but she stopped me. "It's all right, Bob. Really. You've taught me so much. And I really am grateful for all the time you've given me. I love to discuss things with you. I shouldn't have said what I did."

It was hard for me to believe that she was only thirteen. Well, thirteen and a half. She was a young woman and was beginning to think as an adult.

"Virginia, I want to talk in praxeological terms again. But what I have to say is very important and very serious. Frankly, I've carefully avoided this subject until now. But I believe you are mature enough to handle it."

Her big eyes were serene but she was keenly attentive. "Is it about sex?"

"No, hon. We've talked about that, as I'm sure we both remember. However, this is just as serious. Perhaps more so."

"If you say so." She smiled. "But it won't be as interesting. You said so yourself. Nothing competes with sex as an attention-getter."

"Is there something about sex you want to talk about?"

She shook her head. "No. Ever since I had that terrible experience, I feel different about it. You know, then I was just romantic. Of course, in a vague way I knew that men and women are different. And that this difference is sexual, in part. But I thought that it would be so different from what it really is. I just felt a kind of emptiness, a yearning for something I can't explain. And I could hardly get my mind off boys. And for a while, it was only Harvey. But it isn't like that at all any more."

I nodded. "Perfectly normal. Don't you think about sex any more at all?"

"Oh, sure, I do. But it's not in the same way. Sex is very important. But I've accepted an indefinite postponement. And I don't feel deprived at all. Honestly. Isn't that kind of weird in itself? I had such strong urges, Papa. You wouldn't believe. And then we had that talk, and we were both totally open and frank and, well, somehow, the pressure got relieved. I know that one day I will have a total relationship with someone. Maybe a husband. Maybe not. I'm still not sure about that. But I'm no longer interested in sex as a kind of personal experiment. I'm going to have to care a very great deal for a man before he touches me in that way. You can be very sure of that, Papa."

"I'm very happy to hear it, Gigi. Then you are ready to think about something else right now."

"I sure am. Of course, in my novel my heroine is all hung up about sex. But she's going to be a wonderful person, just the same. She'll have loads and loads of men friends but I'm going to make her pure at the same time."

"You'll have to show it to me when you're ready."

"Would you like to read it? That would be terrific! I'd love to have you read it."

"When you're ready. Now, sweetie, I want to talk to you about the inescapable conclusion of praxeological study. Not that every economist or every praxeologist reaches this conclusion. Or if he does, only a very few will admit it. At least in public. So, in a sense, I'm relying on the maturity of your judgment. Exercise care and discretion when you talk to others about what I am going to say.

"Please understand. I'm not trying to censor you or invoke a gag rule. Nothing of the kind. I simply want you to grasp that most people won't be ready to understand what I'm about to reveal. But I think you will. And we always have a temptation to believe that whatever we understand, others will understand. That isn't always true.

"You may recall that at one time I said something to you about communication. How people communicate with each other. You know what happens with most of us? We study something and finally reach a conclusion about it. Then we are eager to tell others what our conclusion is. Actually, that's not a particularly smart way to communicate.

"When we tell our conclusions to someone else, he usually doesn't know how we reached that conclusion. And if he's never followed that particular line of thought, he's apt to think that we are way off base.

"Watch people talking. Listen to them. Mr. A approaches Mr. B. 'What do you think of such and such?' he asks. He's asking for a conclusion on the part of Mr. B. So, Mr. B responds. 'I think this or that.' Immediately, an argument ensues. Mr. A, by one line of reasoning, has reached Conclusion X. Mr. B, by quite another line of reasoning, has reached Conclusion Y. They aren't going to agree because the data each is using are different. They add up to different results. Mr. A and Mr. B frequently part, each marveling how the other can be so mistaken.

"So, here's what I'm getting at. Rather than throwing your conclusions around, begin your communication with data; with facts. Don't start communicating with the end product of your thought, begin with primary information. Add additional facts as the other party is ready for them. Now you'll be communicating and the chance of a major break-off in communication is frequently avoided."

"Is this how you've been communicating with me, Papa?"

"Certainly. To the best of my ability."

"How can you tell when the other person is ready for additional information?"

"This is an important secret about effective communication, Virginia. You have to be patient enough to listen to feedback from him — not to argue in rebuttal, but to gain a glimpse into how *he* sees things. When you communicate that you understand his point of view, then he will be more receptive to further information from you.

"Of course, you have to remember that everybody has a 'hot button.' That means a subject that to him is taboo. If you begin talking about that subject, he immediately reacts emotionally. That should serve as a warning. If you value your communication with that person, better get onto another subject. In that case, it might be good to find out what his conclusions are in that area so you avoid antagonizing him needlessly.

"As I'm sure you know, there are several subjects that tend to tie into 'hot buttons' with lots of people. Economics itself has a number of 'hot buttons' with many. Some people have reached conclusions which simply aren't warranted by the facts. And if you talk about these things, you can be sure of an emotional rejection. Even if you're right, your argument will be rejected because people don't like it. Most people believe what they like; what they want to believe. They don't mean to be this way, frequently, but their values are more meaningful to them than facts you might marshal in opposition."

Virginia bounced in her chair in agreement. "Oh, I know about that, Papa. Remember Mr. Olafson, my Social Science teacher? He was like that."

"And maybe, at that time, so were you?"

Virginia paused, then nodded in agreement. "Yes. I was, too. I see that now. I was throwing my conclusions at him and he was throwing his at me. And we were getting madder and madder by the second. Oh, yes. And it happened with Henry, too. I see what you mean."

"Here's something else to keep in mind. In a 'hot button' area which we conventionally call 'controversial' since there are strong emotional commitments, most people are eager to discuss things provided you *agree* with their conclusions. In these areas, your *conclusions* are more important to your listener than facts. He demands agreement. Possibly the hottest of all hot buttons is religion."

She laughed. "Oh, that is so true. Boy, oh, boy! People are really hung up in that area, Papa. You have to agree on every single point! If you don't, they get mad at you. And they say terrible things to you if you ask questions or seem to disagree with them in the slightest."

"Good. That's exactly what I mean. When people agree on a religion right down the line, they tend to become very clannish. They form an 'in' group and they even have special language and special code words that tell them when they have found a simpatico. Someone who agrees. Everyone else is an outsider."

"I sure know about that, Papa. And it's funny. People who say they are atheists are just as emotionally hung up. They get all emotional if they think someone has a religion. They accuse church people about being hung up, but they have the same symptoms and are just as hung up."

I laughed. "Excellent. Excellent. You are a keen observer, hon. So, religion is a 'hot button' area and it's a good idea to learn where another person's most compelling conclusions are so that you avoid offending him. Either that, or you have to give up communicating with him. Isn't that right?"

"Boy, it sure is."

"Sex is another area that's 'hot,' Virginia. Many people have very strong emotional hang-ups in this area. They are profoundly sure of themselves. And equally sure that any difference of view is in error. And don't just say that it's the adults. Young people are just as sure of themselves, often thinking that an adult has had little sexual knowledge or experience and must, therefore, belong to another species. And whatever has sexual connotations falls into this same 'hot' area. Subjects like abortion, pornography, and even women's lib often draw the emotional ire of antagonists and protagonists alike. So it's good, if you wish to maintain open communication, to learn as many facts as you can and to communicate in the area of facts and not in the area of conclusions. Right?"

"Papa, that is very wise. I see what you mean."

"Of course, hon, if there is some particular conclusion that you think is right, I'm not suggesting that you bottle it up. Just keep in mind that other people have minds which they want to use. When you throw a conclusion at a friend, you are, in a sense, suggesting that he doesn't have to think, you've done his thinking for him. So you might respect the other person's ability to think, and offer him some facts from which to think. It keeps the channels open."

Virginia's eyes shone as she nodded emphatically.

"Splendid. Now, hon, there's another 'hot button' area that I want to discuss with you. Politics."

Virginia squirmed in eagerness. "Oh, great. Papa, that's wonderful. I've been wondering about that. Mr. Olafson has been talking about politics a lot. And I haven't agreed with lots of things he has said, but I've been trying to learn, so I've done as you said. I've listened. And sometimes I've asked him to make a point over again to be sure I understand what he means. But I haven't challenged him, because I really don't know much about it."

"Very wise of you, hon. Most people approach politics from a partisan point of view. And if you challenge them, the reaction is very much like a religious reaction. Each party has a kind of catechism and there is a clannishness about them. Members of each party claim all virtue for their own position and for the elected representatives of their own party. Similarly, they contend that all members of another party are scoundrels who are betraying the country, the Constitution, or the American public."

"Mr. Olafson is pretty good in this area, Papa. That's sort of what he says. He indicates that politics is . . . let's see, how did he say it? He said that politics is the 'science of the possible.' That didn't sound too good to me. But that's what he said it was."

"I see. What does that mean to you?"

"Well, it means that politics is the science of getting whatever you want that's possible to get."

"That's about right, hon. And how does Mr. Olafson say you get what you want through political action?"

"Well, you get organized. You get a big organization with lots of voters and then you demonstrate and show that an awful lot of people support what you want and then the government will do what you ask. That way, you can get whatever you want."

"And you don't like that?"

"Well, it's not very moral. Is it, Papa? It doesn't seem right to me."

"It's not necessarily right in a moral sense, Virginia. But it certainly is correct in the sense that the method you've described gets things done in any kind of country that uses the democratic process."

"There's one girl in my Social Science class who is a Republican. And she's always fighting with Mr. Olafson. I think her father is some kind of elected official. I don't know what he does, but this is sure her 'hot' area. Boy, oh, boy. She goes after Mr. Olafson all the time, and he goes after her, too."

"I suspect that Mr. Olafson is a Democrat."

"Of course. And most of the kids are. But Susie isn't. And she lays into them all pretty good. She's smart."

"And you stay out of it?"

"In Social Science I'm a real cool cat."

"I see. That's good. This way, you can remain in communication with both sides without tipping your own hand. But if someone asks you whether you're a Republican or a

Democrat, what do you say?"

"Oh, I just change the subject and say I haven't made up my mind."

"Fair enough. This is the area I want to discuss with you."

"You're a Republican, aren't you?"

"No. I'm not partisan. I don't belong to either party."

"Then you're an Independent."

"Not even that."

"Oh?"

"I'm someone who thinks praxeologically. And that makes me rather a-political."

"What does that mean?"

"It means that I'm not inclined toward politics at all."

"Papa, do you mind if I contradict you? I think you're a Republican. Maybe you don't belong to any party, but I think you really are, deep down inside. I know that Susie agrees with lots of the things you say."

I nodded. "I know why you might think that way, hon. Republicans often place great emphasis upon private property, and so do I. But I still wouldn't care to advance the concept of a free market and private property by using political methods. So I have some very serious questions about Republican politics."

Virginia nodded. "That's good. So do I. After what's happened recently in Washington, I think lots of the kids have some pretty serious questions about politics. But most of them agree with Mr. Olafson. If you don't like what is going on, the best thing is to organize a big pressure group and bring about some changes."

"And that's what I don't agree with, hon. In virtually all political contests that's what is involved. Each group is trying to get its own concepts of 'the good' — whatever that may be — into law so that those who disagree can be forced into a mold that the pressurizers happen to like. So the political method which is now almost universally extolled in this whole world is essentially what Mr. Olafson says it is. It's the study of what you can do to get everyone else lined up on your side of the fence. You begin with those who can be persuaded. You end by using force on the total."

"Yeah." Virginia's expression was grave. "I keep seeing

that. And I don't like it."

"Have you talked about this to any of your associates?"

"Oh, sure. And the kids see it. But what else can you do? We've got to have a government. And we sure don't want to go back and get a king. Or a dictator. So what else is there? You have to let the people decide. But then they put on the pressure the same way a king or a dictator does."

"Vox populi, vox dei."

"What?"

"It's a Latin phrase. 'The voice of the people is the voice of God.' "

"Is that a religion?"

"No. It's politics. But politics and religion are very close together. They spring from the same root. Those in charge of a religion set down a number of laws or canons or church rules. You are supposed to refrain from doing certain things. If you disobey, the religious person says, God will punish you in the hereafter.

"In politics, the same thing is done. A list of prohibitions is prepared. But it's much more. There is also a growing list of positive commandments, things you are compelled to do. But unlike the religious person, the politician says that if you disobey what he tells you to do, he will punish you here and now.

"In a sense, political governments spring from the doubt that men have of the practical carrying out of God's anger. So they don't trust God to provide the punishment they want to inflict on others. Government punishes here and now."

Virginia squealed in delight. "Oh, that's it! That's it! People really are bitchy about things like that, aren't they? They want those who do things they shouldn't to be hurt."

"I'm afraid so, hon."

"I guess they think that nobody will ever learn."

"Sometimes. They sit in judgment on the behavior of others. Instead of minding their own business, they intrude in the business of others. And they constantly express a moralistic hope of vengeance."

"But, Papa, it is necessary, isn't it? I mean there are bad things that people can do. They can steal and they can rape and they can murder each other. And you can't just let people do things like that and get away with it. I mean, you can't, can you?"

"No, hon, of course not. People must learn not to do things like that."

"So, you have to have a government." She shrugged. "I think it's evil. And I even think that Mr. Olafson thinks it's evil. But he's all for it. So I really don't know what to think."

"All right, hon. Now, let's put that aside for a moment and go back to what I said before about the law of supply and demand."

"What has that got to do with it?"

"I'll see if I can bring it in. But before I do, I want you to achieve a truly detached position. I think this is what most people fail to do when they look at politics. It's the same thing when they look at religion. They're too personally involved. They abandon the objective. It's all terribly, terribly subjective. Most people either love or hate politicians. There's no middle ground.

"So, I want you to imagine that you and I belong to a different race of beings altogether. We've just arrived here on Terra Firma in a spaceship from a planet in another galaxy. We're not involved here at all. So we can take a detached look at what is happening.

"Let's suppose we spend several years studying what's going on here. We're invisible, let's imagine. So we are able to move around to examine people and their behavior without interference. And we see them dealing with the natural resources of this planet, making things, distributing things, using them, and using them up. And we look at their governments and see what their governments are doing. But we aren't involved. So we aren't angry with politicians of either party. We aren't any more angry than a scientist would be angry with a crocodile if he wanted to study crocodile behavior. You don't get angry at a specimen for being what it is. You study it and learn what it is, but you aren't personally involved. Whatever it does, it won't have to affect you, provided only that you don't interfere.

"That's the attitude I want you to have."

"Papa, that's exciting. I can imagine that easy."

"Splendid. So now we've spent quite a few years studying people and their various business and political organizations. What have we learned?"

"Well, we've learned a lot of geography, that's sure."

"Yes, but we've also learned a lot about the economy of this planet. We know there isn't enough of anything and that what there is, is unequally divided. And we see some people doing their best to provide more by productive effort. And we see certain things about people. Some people are good-selfish and some people are bad-selfish. But they're all selfish. And we see that those who are good-selfish are helping themselves by helping others. And we see those who are bad-selfish helping themselves by interfering with others. Now, what do we see governments doing?"

Virginia thought a moment. "Papa, governments are bad-selfish. They always interfere with others. But sometimes those they interfere with are bad-selfish, too."

"Well, why are governments created, then?"

"To do evil things."

"No, hon. I agree with you that they do evil things. But they are created to do good. Remember the profit motive, the drive for plus-factors. The men who create government and who get into government want to do good things. Remember, this is universal about all the people we have studied. It is their primary characteristic. They want the good."

"That doesn't make much sense. If they want the good, why do they create a government which does evil?"

"Ah, that's the real riddle of the Sphinx, my dear. The people in government are dependent upon their popularity. They have to win reputations as being 'good.' So they do all they can to show how loving and how generous and how kind they are. And they promise everyone that if they obtain power, they will do nothing but 'good.' "

"Yes, that's really true. I guess they're all just a bunch of liars."

"In a sense we all are, Gigi. We don't mean to be but it's almost impossible to avoid telling things that aren't so from time to time. We promise things we can't deliver. We see a problem. We hope to solve it. So we say we will. Most of all, we want to convince everyone of our good intentions."

"Papa, there have been an awful lot of lies told by politicians."

"I can't deny it. But it would be wrong of us to assume that politicians are bad people. Just as it would be wrong for us to assume that businessmen are good people. People are people. We're all mixtures of the good and bad. Now, we all *want* the good. But wanting it and delivering it aren't the same thing."

"You're not helping me, Papa. It really is a riddle."

"Remember the man we saw on the beach, Virginia. I told you that even if he drove a getaway car for a bunch of gangsters, he was, at heart, a good man. And when you took Loy's ring, I refused to believe that you were a 'bad' person although you insisted you were. You had done a bad thing. And perhaps that man on the beach had done some bad things, too. Everyone does. A businessman isn't perfect. He makes mistakes. He may do bad things. A politician isn't perfect, either. He makes mistakes. He does bad things."

Virginia shrugged and waved her arms. "Then I guess there's no help for it. We're in a mess."

I chuckled. "That's true. We're in a mess. We have, in fact, exactly the amount and kind of government we deserve. And we have exactly the amount and kind of economy we deserve, as well. All our human relationships are deserved. We've earned them. That's why we have them."

"Oh, my. Is it hopeless? I mean, are we people just a bunch of crocodiles, maybe?"

"Sometimes we act like crocodiles and that's a fact. But, hon, don't be discouraged. Keep your detached position. Let's accept that people who form government and who become political office holders want the good. Just like everyone else."

"All right. I'm detached again. I'm from another planet."

"Good. Now, let's take a look at a government. Imagine, if you will, a group of people inhabiting a large area and they don't have a government. But some of the people become concerned about the bad-selfish people who exist. There always appear to be a few of them. Not a great many, but a few. And they always are a problem.

"So, the concerned people want to do good. They come up with the idea of creating an organization which will use force on those who might act in bad-selfish ways. They set down a list of rules that ought to be obeyed. And they promise to punish anyone who doesn't obey the rules."

"That's just it, Papa. That's the way it is."

"What do the people do when they have this organization?"

"Which people?"

"Well, let's take the people outside of government. What do they do?"

"Why, I guess they go back to producing things and making a living."

"Of course. And they shift responsibility for their own safety and well-being over to the few men in government."

"I see that."

"And what do the men in government do?"

"Well, they stand guard so that people can go about their business."

"Very good, hon. That's the way it happens — at least in theory. But a very particular, practical thing happens at this point. The men in government don't trust anybody. Of course they know that there are only a few bad-selfish people around. But they don't know which ones are that way. And they can't afford to take a chance. So the first thing they do is to tax everyone for the necessary funds so they can stand guard."

"What's wrong with that?"

"If they had a legitimate service to sell, they could create a protective agency and sell their services. Just like anyone else in business. In short, they'd be businessmen, selling protection as a service, to those who believe they ought to have it. They'd probably make a lot of money if they did that."

"Well, isn't that just what the government does?"

"No, hon. Think more closely. The government doesn't simply post a price and ask those who want the service to pay. They levy a tax and collect it from everyone. You see, they reason that the bad-selfish person wouldn't be willing to pay for their services. But they don't know who is bad-selfish. So they insist that *everyone* pay the price. When an agency or organization does that, it is no longer a business, it becomes a government. When services are sold in the market place, the buyer can purchase or not as he pleases. But when you set up a government, no one can turn down the services offered. Everyone is compelled to pay."

"How else could you get the bad-selfish person to pay?"

"Good question. Probably you couldn't."

"Then what's wrong with it?"

"Here's what's wrong with it, hon. When the government forces everyone to pay, the government presently concludes that anyone who doesn't pay is bad-selfish. Therefore, they will treat the man who doesn't pay his taxes in exactly the same way they would if he had robbed a bank."

"That's true."

"The government concludes that what they call 'the law' is the final authority. So government doesn't really try to protect the people; instead, it tries to enforce the law."

"Isn't that the same thing?"

"No, it isn't, hon. For once the people in government find that the public at large is shifting responsibility to them and that they have the power to collect any sum of money whatever, then the people in government, hoping to win fine reputations for doing good, begin to collect more and more money so they can do more and more things with it. And they come up with more and more programs. And that requires more and more money. Presently, the people are bowed under a weight of taxation and government debt that becomes intolerable. But they don't know what to do about it. They imagine that if government weren't there, they would be unprotected. The fact is that they are not at all protected from their government, which takes more from them than is stolen by all the thieves and crooks outside of government."

"Oh, my. I see why you call it the 'riddle of the Sphinx.' "

"Right. Now, how do we cut through this Gordian knot?"

"What's that, Papa?"

"Well, it's a knot that appears in an ancient Greek myth. A certain ruler, warned by an oracle that anyone who could untie a certain knot would one day conquer him, did everything in his power to make it impossible to untie that knot. The story has it that Alexander the Great cut the knot with his sword. Since then, a Gordian knot has become a figure of speech. It means a riddle that is almost impossible to solve."

"Is that what you mean, Papa? Do we have to cut the knot with a sword?"

"Some people think so, but I don't. Symbolically, I would suppose that this would mean that to get rid of the evils of government, we would have to create a power great enough to overthrow that government by the sword, or with force. It's happened many times in history. But the result is always the same. In order to overthrow a government by force, it is necessary to create a focal point of force that is more powerful than the government to be overthrown. The people in that focal point, interpreting their own actions as 'good,' now try to become even more powerful to prevent someone from doing the same thing to them. So governments grow and grow, and each revolution that topples a given government tends to create another one, often worse than the one that was overthrown."

"Okay, Papa. You're very smart. Can you untie the knot?"

"I'm not at all sure, but I think I see where one of the ends of the knotted cord is located."

"I'd sure like to see that."

"All right. Let's look at it this way. People want to be protected, right? We are sensitive creatures, responsive to pleasure and to pain. We don't want pain to be inflicted on us. And any time one of our boundaries is crossed against our will, we experience pain of one sort or another. That's true, isn't it?"

"Yes. I remember that. That's true."

"So we seek to avoid pain and to acquire good, gain, profit, whatever you want to call it. Plus-factors of one sort or another."

"Yes, go on."

"But government isn't really organized to protect us from pain. It is organized not to act but to re-act. What the government does is to provide a list of rules, do's and don'ts. And then it waits. And if someone is injured, then the government acts to catch the person who has inflicted injury and to inflict injury on him, in turn."

"But that's how it has to be."

"I don't think so. But I think this is what we've been conditioned to believe over many long years of shifting responsibility over to government. Government is organized to retaliate, not to protect. And these are opposite concepts.

"You see, hon, if you have to retaliate against someone who has injured you, it is quite clear that you weren't protected. If you were protected in fact, retaliation would be impossible. Retaliation and protection are opposites. If you are protected in fact, retaliation is impossible. If you believe you have to retaliate, it is only because you were not protected."

Virginia stood up. "Oh! Oh, Papa! I *do* see that. It's kind of hard but I see it!"

"Sit down, hon. Thank you. It isn't everyone that can readily get that distinction, but it is an important one. You see, the way the government is organized, we must *first be injured* before the government can act. And perhaps at one time in the development of human society that was good enough. It was the best we could devise."

"But, Papa, what if a person commits a murder? You can't just let him go free?"

"Wait a minute, hon. You're falling back into the old way of thinking. You have insensibly accepted that protection can't be provided. You have to begin thinking protection. Protection. Protection. Obviously, if a murder has occurred, it's too late to prevent that murder. Murders must be prevented. Retaliation is just a form of vengeance. And it doesn't bring the dead person back to life."

"But, Papa, what if it does happen?"

"No, Virginia. Think the other way. What if you are protected and someone wants to kill you? If you are *really* protected, then you can't retaliate against the person who wants you dead. Nothing has happened. Retaliation is reaction. We must learn to take action before, not after the commission of a crime."

"Oh, I see *that!*"

"Fine. Then, keep in mind as a constant, *if* you prevent

the crime from happening, the question of retaliating can be abandoned. It becomes academic."

She nodded doubtfully. "I suppose so."

"Now put the pieces together thus far. Governments are organized not to prevent crime but to take vengeance after the crime has occurred. Thus, for governments to continue to justify their existence, there must always be a certain level of crime. You and I are the bait in the trap. We are the undefended cheese that lures the criminal rat. After the rat strikes, and only then, will the government act to punish the rat. Because it doesn't know which creature *is* a rat until after the fact. So it presumes that every citizen is a potential rat. But it waits for proof. Meanwhile, the government takes what it likes from all of us, legally committing theft and worse, so that when private illegal theft or worse occurs, it can punish the rat who did it. That puts us in double jeopardy. We are victimized first by the government to get the money, and then later by the private rat who also takes our money or something else that we value."

"So we get it coming and going! But if we were really protected, we wouldn't have to retaliate."

"We not only wouldn't 'have to,' we couldn't. It would be impossible."

"Yes, but that's all theory, Papa. You can't really protect everyone that well."

"Let's consider the effectiveness of protection as opposed to retaliation in a few moments, Virginia. First, I want to make another very important point. Remember, I mentioned the law of supply and demand a bit ago? Let me deal with that now. I drew that scriggly old snake to show how the law of supply and demand works."

"Yes, I remember that very well, Papa. The ocean."

"Right. Now, sometimes we think that there are two groups of people; the businessmen who comprise one group, and the customers who comprise the second."

"Well, there are, aren't there?"

"Not really. While it's true that there are some consumers who aren't business people all the time, or even some of the time, there is no such thing as a business person who is not a consumer. There aren't two groups;

there's just one. Humanity itself. We are all of us consumers as long as we live. And most of us are also productive at least during a major portion of our lives. Some of us produce by using our muscles, some by using our brains, some by using our money or properties. But except for a very few, all of us in the whole world produce a great deal of the time. Of course, when we're very young, we are not able to produce. Or when we are old or sick. But we keep consuming all the time."

"Yes, I see that."

"Good. If the government acted to protect those who want protection, rather than to retaliate in our names, then it would be offering a legitimate service. A great many people would choose to buy it, although some might not. But when government takes on the job of committing vengeance in our name, it must arrogate to itself the power of violating anyone's boundaries. And it does this in any and all ways.

"Keep in mind that when government is first formed, it doesn't have anything. It has no money and no resources. So in order to get the resources to pay government personnel, it imposes a tax upon all. Thus, all that the government does, if you think it through, is to help some at the expense of others. It has nothing of its own."

"But that's true with any business, Papa. You keep reminding me of it. The businessman doesn't have anything, either. He just offers a good or service. But all that he has, he gets from his customers. He doesn't even pay his own taxes."

"True enough. The difference relates to force. Government takes what it wants. The businessman obtains only what customers voluntarily give to him."

"I see that part of it."

"So if government wants to help the victim of a crime, the government does so by injuring everyone else in society in order to help the one."

"Say that again."

I repeated the phrase. "This way, the costs of crime which might have been borne by a single victim are imposed upon everyone else in society. The criminal imposes on his victim and then government imposes on everyone else."

"But that's good, isn't it? That way, the cost of crime isn't so hard on just one person."

"Think again. The victim has already been forced to pay in full by the criminal. Now, in addition, everyone else is forced to pay. And the victim actually pays twice."

"But the victim gets back what the criminal stole."

"In what way, if the crime is a serious one? Granted, if the thief takes your money, you *may* get it back. Government policing efforts aren't very successful in this area but it's comforting to suppose that it will happen. But how do you get back the life of your loved one who is murdered? How do you restore an unmolested condition to the victim of rape? No, hon. When it comes to heinous crimes, not only is the victim made to pay, but everyone else pays, too.

"Now, let's look at some of the other things government does. All it ever really *tries* to do is to protect us one way or another. It provides schools so we are protected from our ignorance. It provides tariff walls to protect businessmen. It helps push up wages so the worker is protected from a low wage. It protects the farmer and the mother and the child. But note how it is done. Think about the law of supply and demand.

"If the government decides to help farmers, what does it do? It taxes the people who live in cities, and then it passes the benefit on to farmers. But how does that help farmers? In order to sell his produce, the farmer has to sell to people in cities. The people in the cities who are taxed find themselves less able to buy what the farmer produces. So the people on whom the farmer must depend are injured in order to help the farmer. That doesn't really help. It hurts. Then, if the government decides to help the people in cities, it taxes the farmer and passes the benefit along. But the people in cities are dependent upon the farmer. If the farmer is injured, how will that help those who must depend on him?

"If the government acts to protect consumers, it does so by taxing producers. But the consumers depend on the producers. If producers are injured, they are less able to provide what consumers want at a low price. Conversely, if the government acts to protect businessmen, it must injure customers. But that doesn't help businessmen. You don't help the businessman by injuring his customers on whom he must depend. Remember, there aren't special groups of consumers and producers. We're all the same."

"Is everything the government does wrong?"

"Hon, every use of force by means of which people are compelled to do what they wouldn't otherwise have done, or are prevented from doing what they normally would do, is wrong. That's what a boundary violation is all about. To prevent a *boundary* violation would certainly be a good thing. But government doesn't really prevent that. However, let me grant that the mere existence of a retaliatory force *may* inhibit a wrongdoer to some degree. But when we examine this agency of government, what happens becomes very clear. If a criminal violates a boundary, government uses this as a reason to violate the boundaries not only of the criminal, if he can be found, but also of all the other men and women who are made to pay for the action. Government doesn't cure problems. It aggravates them.

"In short, hon, to prevent theft, government practices it, legally. To inhibit murder, government practices it, legally. And people know it. They know that government injures them at every turn. They know that an injury to a useful member of society, either a producer or a customer, injures both parties to any transaction. At least they know it if they think about it. But they don't know what to do about it."

"All right, Papa. What's the answer?"

"I'm not sure, my dear. But let's see if we can find the other end of the cord. I think I may be able to. But you must bear in mind that in between the two ends, this cord has been tangled and messed up for thousands of years. So it's really an incredible snarl.

"Every one of us, Gigi, has a limited competence. And that's all. The problems we face are huge. I can't solve them for everyone. That's not possible. Let me see if I can bring this second end of the cord into sight.

"As an adult human, it is my job to earn enough to look after myself. Can I always do that? Not perfectly, my dear. I know what it is to be 'down on my luck'; to be broke, in fact. I lived through the depression of the thirties and it was a rough time for me, I can tell you. But it is up to me. I have a limited competence, but I do have some competence, some capacity. Actually, mine is pretty good. Some aren't as able as I am; others have far more to work with than I have. There is no equality in abilities, as we know.

"But it's up to me. I have enough ability to feed myself and to clothe myself and to house myself. Not perfectly. I've had to miss some meals from time to time. And I've found periods when I got behind in my rent and my car payments. In fact, I one time had a car repossessed because I couldn't finish paying for it. But it was still up to me. And I've often worn old clothes because they were the best I could afford.

"I'll tell you something else. There are no perfect products or services in the market. None. I've never eaten a perfect meal or had a perfect house, or bought a perfect suit. I've never had a car that didn't have something go wrong in it. I've never had a tire that wouldn't go flat. Men in business keep trying to make things better but, thus far, perfection escapes their search. Nothing is perfect."

"That's certainly true."

"Our trouble with government is that it teaches us to shift responsibility to it. When we do, we get the idea that government *has solved* the problem. It hasn't. Gigi, we ought to realize that there are problems we have to live with that we can't solve. We have to keep on working and keep on earning money and keep on eating every day. There are on-going problems that relate to living. We don't solve them. We just manage them well or badly. That's all we can do.

"But government encourages an illusion. Because when we shift a burden to the government, we shift responsibility. And then we can shrug and presume that it isn't a problem any more; *government has solved it*. But that isn't so. The problems of pollution, poverty, shortages, and so on, are the challenges that life offers. We have to live with them and manage them."

"Yes, I see that."

"Fine. So here's the end of the cord. The government pretends that it will deal with problems for *society*. That can't be done. That is an illusion.

"For example, government tries to make *society* safe.

That is impossible. And the statistics illustrate that fact. I've been collecting data on crime for years. The FBI Uniform Crime Reports reveal that with only occasional brief interludes, the problem of crime gets worse and worse all the time."

"I know that's true. They were talking about that in school just the other day."

"So, when we talk about the likelihood of protecting people, as opposed to the likelihood of solving the crime problem by retaliation, we have to begin where we are. And where we are isn't a good place to be. Government is trying to protect society. That is why it has this big hang-up with what it calls 'the law.' The policeman looks at everyone in society as a potential rat. He is hired to enforce the law. Now, if he were hired to protect his customers, that's what he would do.

"In short, government can't feed society, can't clothe society, can't house society, or give medical care to it, or protect it. No one in government and all of government combined can do these things. It's impossible. But the government says it can, so we shift responsibility to it and then marvel that everything gets worse.

"Now, put the pieces together. If you told me that it was my job to protect society, I would have to take so much away from everyone in society in order to hire the necessary manpower to do such a tremendous job that the amount I'd take would be larger than the whole of society could engender without going broke. But I can protect myself. Not perfectly, true. I can't do anything perfectly. But I can protect myself as easily as I can feed myself. Or clothe myself or house myself.

"Gigi, I've lived a lot of years and I've never met a perfect man or one totally competent to manage even his own affairs. We all goof up at times. But I can do a pretty fair job of it, and so can nearly everyone else, provided I limit my activities to looking after myself. This I can manage."

"Papa, we were talking about crime in school. Some of the kids think the cops are crooked. Golly, you read about it all the time. Is that what you mean?"

"No, hon. Not at all. Sure, there may be an occasional

bad apple in the barrel. You can find that anywhere. Let me say on behalf of the nation's police force that I think the men hired for this job are some of the finest men you can find. But they have an impossible job. They are supposed to protect *everybody* from *everybody.* They have to deal at a societal level. And that is the end of the cord in that direction. It can't be done.

"Take the average community of 100,000 people. How many police will be hired to protect that number? Probably at the moment, somewhere between one hundred and seventy-five to two hundred. Let's get carried away. Let's assume that 1,000 are hired as police. There are at least 25,000 homes and 30,000 cars in that town. There are at least 5,000 businesses. And 100,000 people. How could 1,000 well trained, well equipped, totally dedicated men handle that problem? It isn't possible. Anybody can attack anybody at any time. Anyone can be victimized in any way at any time. The police can't be everywhere.

"Besides, keep in mind that the police aren't hired to protect. They are hired to let something happen *first.* Then, after it has been reported, they can act. To get even! And that's the old Babylonian idea of an eye for an eye and a tooth for a tooth. I'll remind you that even the Babylonians learned after awhile that if you practice 'an eye for an eye,' you end up in a town filled with one-eyed men. It doesn't get the results you're after."

Virginia's face had grown grave. She surveyed me with great solemnity. "Papa, I know that what you've said is true. We are really in a mess. How did we ever get started relying on government so much?"

"I have a theory here, Virginia. It's only a theory, and maybe I'm wrong. But let me explain it to you. When we look at the evidence of men living on this planet, we discover them first living in a 'state of nature.' That means that they are very primitive. Their economy is founded on hunting or foraging. They have only a few crude tools. There aren't many of them alive. Life is, as Hobbes put it, 'ugly, brutish, and short.'

"But after many millenia, some men figured out how to plant crops. And we had what could be called an agrarian revolution. We learned to become more productive and life improved. It was at this time that governments were devised. I'll call the epoch I'm talking about the epoch of barbarism. And to make my point I'll say that primitive men — savages, those who live by hunting and foraging — are like the children of our species. They are simple minded, filled with superstition, with virtually no technology at all.

"Then they learn agriculture. At this point in time they invent government, trying to make things better. I'll call this the barbaric period, the period of humanity's teens. Their technology improves. Life is much better for the barbarian, in general, than it is for the savage.

"Keep in mind, sweetheart, that I'm not trying to downgrade teenagers. I am making an analogy, seeing the species itself as passing from childhood into the teen period and, finally, into adulthood. As I view it, adulthood began for a very limited number of people about 500 B.C., or about 2,500 years ago. It was the discovery of writing, the beginning of philosophy and the systematic use of observation, the development of the power of thought, that advanced a few of our species into adulthood as harbingers for the whole species. I see ourselves in that emerging epoch right now.

"Now, the biggest thing going for adults is that they have access to much more information and experience than those who are younger. And it seems to me that men who have found out how to put people on the moon, and to make computers, and to harness the power of the atom, have moved out of their teens."

"You know, that's a funny thing, Papa. Mr. Olafson would agree with you. He sees it the same way."

"Very good. Apparently you have learned a great deal from him, Gigi, even though he may not yet understand economics or praxeology."

"Papa, what can we do? I mean, everything is in such a mess."

"Actually, it really isn't, hon. Changes of this magnitude take time. We must be patient. As I told you earlier, we have the exact kind of government and the exact kind of economy that we've demanded. We created both. We get what we work to provide. What I'd like to suggest is that mankind is on the threshold of a great new breakthrough.

We are going to have to learn how to live without government. Government is now obsolescent if not obsolete. We have to learn to manage our affairs without it.

"Isn't it true, hon, that most people look at government as though it were a big daddy? They expect the men in government to be all-wise and all-powerful. Just in the same way they think about God. The only trouble is that there isn't anyone who fits that bill. So people are constantly disillusioned and hurt. They keep expecting government to be super-human. And then they are heart-broken when events prove them wrong."

"Is our government all wrong, then, Papa?" Her voice broke.

"Sweetheart. It's probably the best that was ever devised. It's just that we, the human species, are growing up. We can see the shortcomings in our big daddy and we don't like it. The early American philosophers glimpsed this when they severed the umbilical cord connecting them with the British monarchy. In the Declaration, they affirmed independence; self-government. The vision dimmed when self-government became confused with political government.

"The time is fast arriving once again when we have to leave the family home, government, and make a life for ourselves. I think that is what is happening to our species as a whole.

"As a matter of fact, that is already happening between you and me. I think it happens at the level of the species, too. As the microcosm, so the macrocosm. You are growing up. There was a time when you thought I was just about perfect. But you've seen me lose my temper. And you've seen me make judgments that were faulty. I'm not perfect. I insisted on that long ago, but you thought otherwise. Now, at last you know it is true. I'm not perfect. No one is. And so you are maturing and one day, I hope not too soon, but surely one day, you will leave us and go out to make your own life. It is the way things have to be.

"You see, the more of my failings that become visible to you, the more you will resolve to do better than I can do. And you will, too. And in time, you may have a son or daughter of your own. Perhaps both. To begin with, they will be totally dependent on you and look up to you as all wise and all good and all powerful. But of course you won't be. But you'll do your best.

"And then they'll see where you, too, have been wrong. And they'll break off and go out on their own.

"As I see it, this is humanity's destiny. Government is like a kind of father. It's a real *big* big daddy. But it's filled with men, sometimes very good and wise men, and without exception they, too, want the good. Of course, some will be bad-selfish and some good-selfish, but that is only to be expected. Finally, as a species, we have to grow up. And no one ever really grows up while he is dependent upon a big daddy. You have to go it alone. It's hard. But that's what we all have to do. Individually, and eventually as a species."

Virginia came over to me. Her approach was soft yet dignified. One hand reached out to touch my cheek. There were tears in her eyes.

"I don't want to leave you, Papa. Not ever. But I know that you have told me the truth. And I do understand what you mean. Golly, it's kind of scary."

"Yes, it is, hon. There's a great big world out there and how we are going to manage without a big daddy, I really don't know. But we're going to have to do it. Somehow, sometime, we're going to have to put away our teenage toys. They don't work too well and we must abandon them for something that comes closer to dealing with the reality of man."

She nodded in silence.

I opened a desk drawer and turned off a switch. "Virginia, I have taped our conversation. I thought you might like to go over it again, perhaps more than once. So I've made a tape cassette and want you to have it."

I took it out of the machine and handed it to her.

"Thank you. But I don't have . . . . "

I interrupted. "If you'll take that box off the bookshelf and open it, you'll find a cassette player. It's for you. And you can play music on it, too. Anything you like."

"Oh! Why, thank you, Papa. I didn't expect a present."

"That's what made it so much fun for me to buy. I've given you quite a bit to think about. And of course I'll be happy to talk more about economics or praxeology with you any time."

I watched as she left my office. I hoped I had said the right things. Of course she was terribly young. But life is no laggard and time sweeps on its inexorable way. I could unravel the cord for myself. But there must be a significant number of persons capable of doing the same thing before it will stretch out to its full length, and thus span future ages.

BOOKS BY BOB LeFEVRE

JUSTICE

THE LIBERTARIAN

THIS BREAD IS MINE

THE PHILOSOPHY OF OWNERSHIP

THE NATURE OF MAN AND HIS GOVERNMENT

THE POWER OF CONGRESS (edited by R.S. Radford)

CONSTITUTIONAL GOVERNMENT TODAY IN SOVIET RUSSIA

LeFEVRE'S JOURNAL
a quarterly

PINE TREE PRESS, Box 2353, Orange, CA 92669